Real World Web Services

Other Java™ resources from O'Reilly

Related titles

Java™ in a Nutshell
Java™ and XML
Java Servlet and JSP Cookbook™
Java™ Web Services in a Nutshell

Learning Java™
Head First Java™
Google Hacks™
eBay Hacks™
PayPal Hacks™

Java Books Resource Center

java.oreilly.com is a complete catalog of O'Reilly's books on Java and related technologies, including sample chapters and code examples.

OnJava.com is a one-stop resource for enterprise Java developers, featuring news, code recipes, interviews, weblogs, and more.

Conferences

O'Reilly brings diverse innovators together to nurture the ideas that spark revolutionary industries. We specialize in documenting the latest tools and systems, translating the innovator's knowledge into useful skills for those in the trenches. Visit *conferences.oreilly.com* for our upcoming events.

Safari Bookshelf (*safari.oreilly.com*) is the premier online reference library for programmers and IT professionals. Conduct searches across more than 1,000 books. Subscribers can zero in on answers to time-critical questions in a matter of seconds. Read the books on your Bookshelf from cover to cover or simply flip to the page you need. Try it today with a free trial.

Real World Web Services

Will Iverson

O'REILLY®

Beijing · Cambridge · Farnham · Köln · Paris · Sebastopol · Taipei · Tokyo

Real World Web Services
by Will Iverson

Copyright © 2005 O'Reilly Media, Inc. All rights reserved.
Printed in the United States of America.

Published by O'Reilly Media, Inc., 1005 Gravenstein Highway North, Sebastopol, CA 95472.

O'Reilly books may be purchased for educational, business, or sales promotional use. Online editions are also available for most titles (*safari.oreilly.com*). For more information, contact our corporate/institutional sales department: (800) 998-9938 or *corporate@oreilly.com*.

Editor:	Brett D. McLaughlin
Production Editor:	Mary Anne Weeks Mayo
Cover Designer:	Ellie Volckhausen
Interior Designer:	Melanie Wang

Printing History:

October 2004:	First Edition.

RepKover.™ This book uses RepKover,™ a durable and flexible lay-flat binding.

ISBN: 0-596-00642-X

[M]

Table of Contents

Preface

The core idea behind this book is simple: after years of hype, what are the major players *really* doing with web services? Standard bodies may wrangle and platform vendors may preach, but what technologies are actually in use?

Think of this book as a field guide to the wild and woolly world of nontrivial deployed web services. The heart of the book is a series of projects that demonstrate the use and integration of Google, Amazon, eBay, PayPal, FedEx, and many more web services. Some of these vendors have been extremely successful with their web service deployments; for example, eBay processes over a *billion* web service requests a month.

Not all web services are created equal: some rely on a variety of strange formats; others require extensive and error-prone XML; and still others require a minimal knowledge of SOAP and WSDL. This book provides compelling examples of the value of SOAP and WSDL for the client developer. In Chapter 4, for example, you can compare the custom bindings required for working with complex XML data types against the generation of SOAP binding generation from WSDL.

Organization

This book is divided into four sections: introductory material, a conceptual orientation with regard to web services, the various projects surveying real world web service deployments, and finally, a brief chapter outlining some thoughts on the future of web services. While experienced developers may be inclined to skim the introductory chapters, it may be worth covering them again just to make sure you haven't missed the forest for the trees.

Chapter 1, *Web Service Evolution*

> This chapter provides a high level, business-oriented introduction to web services. Technology serves human needs, and this chapter shows how web services fill an important role in the development of the Web. Many developers

may be familiar with these concepts already, but it is as important to explain *why* you do a thing as to explain how it is done.

Chapter 2, *Foundations of Web Services*
While Chapter 1 covers a business-oriented approach to the history of web services, this chapter provides a technical history. Seasoned developers may find this all familiar, but for readers just joining the web services conversation, this is vital background information. In addition, this chapter can serve as a useful checklist for planning your own web service development and deployment plans.

Chapter 3, *Development Platform*
This chapter provides an introduction to the Java™ development platform and tools used in the projects in this book. An introduction is given to Apache Tomcat, Apache XML-RPC, and Apache Axis, the web server, XML-RPC, and SOAP/WSDL toolkits respectively. Obviously, Java is not the only development platform available, and a brief discussion of alternatives concludes the chapter.

Chapter 4, *Project 1: Competitive Analysis*
The first project in the book, this chapter shows how data from Amazon, eBay, and Google can be used to present an integrated report to a user. Connectivity to each of these three web service providers is shown, providing an example of the developer effort required to access each system.

Chapter 5, *Project 2: Auctions and Shipping*
This chapter shows how FedEx and eBay can be integrated to provide auction listings with precalculated FedEx shipping estimates. XML is used throughout—from the local auction listings to FedEx and eBay web services.

Chapter 6, *Project 3: Billing and Faxing*
In this chapter, high-tech web services are used to integrate PayPal billing with low-tech fax technology.

Chapter 7, *Project 4: Syndicated Search*
This chapter illustrates a web service gateway, using a Google search result to provide a syndicated RSS feed.

Chapter 8, *Project 5: News Aggregator*
While other examples in this book operate in direct response to user interaction, this chapter uses the Quartz scheduler framework to monitor Amazon, eBay, Google, and RSS feeds on a regular, reliable schedule.

Chapter 9, *Project 6: Audio CD Catalog*
This chapters shows how CDDB and Amazon can be used together to create a catalog of your audio CDs.

Chapter 10, *Project 7: Hot News Sheet*
In this chapter, you'll build an application using RSS to provide a single web page showing what's hot both from the mainstream news and the weblog universe, side by side. The application will additionally fold in results from a Google search on these topics for yet another angle on the news.

Chapter 11, *Project 8: Automatic Daily Discussions*
> In this chapter, you'll build an application to combine your Blogger or LiveJournal weblog with Google's search functionality to create automatic prompts for daily discussions.

Chapter 12, *Future Web Service Directions*
> This chapter starts with a look at some of the more futuristic web service technologies, including REST, UDDI, Rendezvous, and BPEL/BPEL4WS. A look at the future of web service development follows, which considers ease-of-use, the need for a business model, security, and finally, the consolidation of web services.

Conventions Used in This Book

The following font conventions are used in this book:

Italic is used for:

- Unix pathnames, filenames, and program names
- Internet addresses, such as domain names and URLs
- New terms where they are defined

Boldface is used for:

- Names of GUI items (window names, buttons, menu choices, etc.)

`Constant width` is used for:

- Command lines and options that should be typed verbatim
- Names and keywords in Java programs, including method names, variable names, and class names
- XML element names and tags, attribute names, and other XML constructs that appear as they would within an XML document

 Indicates a tip, suggestion, or general note.

 Indicates a warning or caution.

Using Code Examples

This book is here to help you get your job done. In general, you may use the code in this book in your programs and documentation. You do not need to contact us for permission unless you're reproducing a significant portion of the code. For example, writing a program that uses several chunks of code from this book does not require permission. Selling or distributing a CD-ROM of examples from O'Reilly books *does* require permission. Answering a question by citing this book and quoting example code does not require permission. Incorporating a significant amount of example code from this book into your product's documentation *does* require permission.

We appreciate, but don't require, attribution. An attribution usually includes the title, author, publisher, and ISBN. For example: "*Real World Web Services*, by Will Iverson. Copyright 2004 O'Reilly Media, Inc., 0-596-00642-X."

If you feel your use of code examples falls outside fair use or the permission given here, feel free to contact us at *permissions@oreilly.com*.

Comments and Questions

Please address comments and questions concerning this book to the publisher:

> O'Reilly Media, Inc.
> 1005 Gravenstein Highway North
> Sebastopol, CA 95472
> 800-998-9938 (in the U.S. or Canada)
> 707-829-0515 (international or local)
> 707-829-0104 (fax)

There is a web page for this book, which lists errata, examples, and additional information. You can access this page at:

> *http://www.oreilly.com/catalog/realwws*

To comment or ask technical questions about this book, send email to:

> *bookquestions@oreilly.com*

For more information about books, conferences, Resource Centers, and the O'Reilly Network, see the O'Reilly web site at:

> *http://www.oreilly.com*

Acknowledgments

First, I must send my gratitude to the unseen engine behind the production, marketing, and sales of this book. I know you're there and appreciate all your efforts. Thanks to everyone who has contributed in one form or another to the technologies underlying and comprising web services. We so blithely take for granted so much of this innovation—we stand on the shoulders of giants.

This book wouldn't be what it is without the efforts of my editor, Brett McLaughlin. His work made for a far better book. Thanks to Tim O'Reilly for all the fine tomes that grace my bookshelf and for allowing me to add a second title to O'Reilly's excellent library. For their time, enthusiasm, and professional support, I would like to thank Brian Lawley and Daniel Steinberg. Has it really been that long?

On a personal note, thanks to friends and family for their support. And finally, thanks to Mom, Diane, and Cynthia. You are, quite simply, the best.

CHAPTER 1

Web Service Evolution

What are web services? While this might seem a simple question, this book demonstrates that the query has many answers. Much of this is because the typical conversation about web services suffers from the blending of several distinct concepts. Most software developers focus on the technical underpinnings that make communication possible (such as SOAP and XML-RPC). Others add to the web services category developer infrastructure, such as WSDL, the Web Services Description Language. Some even include a wide host of other pieces, including a mind-numbing array of standards (some real, some theoretical).

Because of this confusion, we must define what is meant by the term *web services*. Here's a good start:

> Web Services: A vague term that refers to distributed or virtual applications or processes that use the Internet to link activities or software components. A travel Web site that takes a reservation from a customer, and then sends a message to a hotel application, accessed via the Web, to determine if a room is available, books it, and tells the customer he or she has a reservation is an example of a Web Services application.
>
> *—Business Process Trends*
> *http://www.bptrends.com/resources_glossary.*
> *cfm?letterFilter=W&displayMode=all*

This is a great start, but it still needs to be clarified a bit. This book doesn't engage in an intellectual debate as to the "correctness" of web services on a theological level. Instead, it focuses on the practical, real world usage of web services. For this book's purposes, web services are the latest evolution in distributed computing, allowing for structured communication via Internet protocols. As you'll see, this includes everything from sending HTTP GET commands to retrieving an XML document through the use of SOAP and various vendor SDKs.

Client/Server Origins

Most developers are familiar with the basic concept of client/server computing: a central server handles requests from one or more clients. It's the foundation of the Web as described by HTTP and HTML: a web server sends pages to a browser client.

As shown in Figure 1-1, you can see that the client browser initiates the request, which is then processed and responded to by the web server.

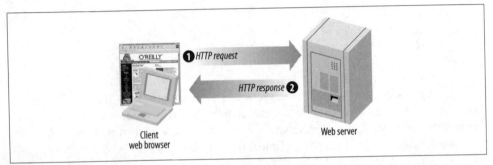

Figure 1-1. Web concept of client server

Before the Web really took off, the term client/server was used to describe something slightly different—a central database server that was accessed by custom clients (often written in Visual Basic, C, Pascal, or other languages). Nobody really wanted to run around, constantly installing and reinstalling these custom clients every time there was a bug to be fixed, so people quickly started hooking up smarter, more sophisticated web servers to databases. In order to distinguish these smarter web servers from "dumb" web servers (that served mainly static files), the term *application server* become popular (in some circles, you'll hear the term *web container* used as well, usually when the server does a lot more than just handle web data).

As you can see in Figure 1-2, the notion of a client and a server becomes more complex in these systems, often called *three-tier systems*. The browser is clearly acting as a client of the application server, but the application server is a client of the database. In effect, the application server is acting both as a client of the database and a server for the client browser.

Consider the system shown in Figure 1-3: note the number of connections, and the number of different roles (client and server) being played by the different systems. These more complex systems are referred to as *n-tier systems*, because they can have any number of tiers.

As a mental exercise, consider the following:

- How do you debug this system?
- Each network connection implies a certain latency and bandwidth overhead. How many connections are appropriate? What happens to the rest of the system if one machine "starves" another by using all its bandwidth or available connections?

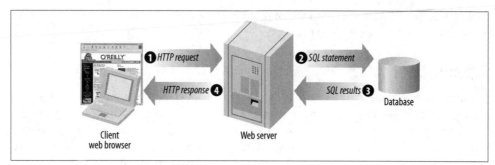

Figure 1-2. Three-tier web system

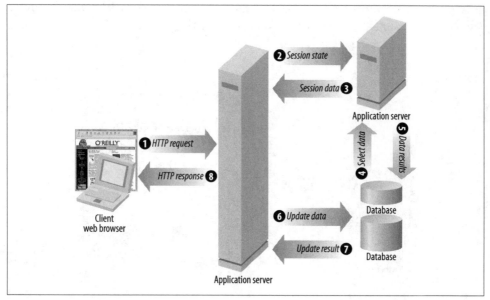

Figure 1-3. An N-Tier system

- How are these connections secured?
- What happens if one or more systems crash or otherwise become unavailable?
- How do you roll out new applications?

These are tricky problems. When you're working with web services, you'll want to keep these potential pitfalls in mind.

The Undefined Web

The concept of a browser talking to a web server is perhaps the most popular client/server system devised (email is the other major one). It didn't take very long before the popularity of this model lead to some interesting questions about the proper relationship between the client and the server.

Scraping Data

A couple of web sites, desperate for content, realized that they could *scrape* the HTML of other sites and display some or all of that information in a different format. For example, let's say that you ran a small web site devoted to the glories of Davis, CA. As shown in Figure 1-4, you set up a site that grabs the weather report from another site (steps 2 and 3) and then grabs the stock quote for the public corporation that runs the local gas station (steps 4 and 5). The user can visit your site and get your information as well as the data from the other two sites as well; throw a banner ad at the top of the page, and you'll soon be rich!

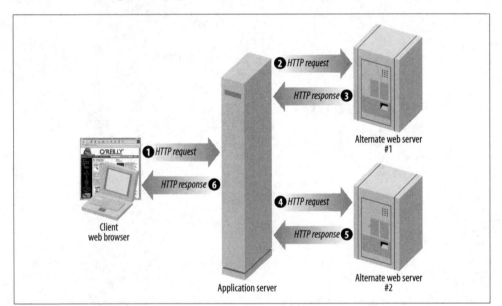

Figure 1-4. An application server scraping other sites

The problem with scraping (dubious ethics aside) is that HTML is extremely fragile. The only promise given with HTML is that a browser can render properly formatted HTML in a human-readable format, and even that's a bit of a reach sometimes. A very minor formatting change can break your HTML parser, and the operator of the site doesn't care (or is actively trying to foil your attempts to steal content).

Now, let's take this to the next logical step. Let's say the weather and stock guys notice that you're reading their data, and both call you and generously offer to trade you legitimate access to their data in exchange for links back to their site. You agree, and now you need to set this up. The immediate question becomes: what standards and specifications do you use to tie all this information together?

This is perhaps one of the most contentious and controversial aspects of web services. How do you decide the actual implementation details for how these systems are going to talk to each other?

The Dangers of Vendor Lock In

Most developers who have worked in the field for a while have lumps of code that are, for one reason or another, no longer viable. Common reasons include a shift in the popularity of given programming languages, changes in the market share or architecture of software platforms, or the release of new operating systems. Regardless of the reason, it's a painful day when you wake up and realize that your 300,000-line, lovingly hand-crafted Pascal code for Mac OS 7 is now essentially worthless, or that you'll never find anyone to help maintain those 28,000 lines of your favorite assembly program. That fear of platform lock in—you wake up one day and find that your code is now worthless because the vendor that provided the service has gone out of business—is a pretty powerful reason to delay adding web service consumption to your list of features.

As we work our way through the examples in this book, I'll note possible failure areas for vendors and strategies for dealing with these problems.

Fragile Interdependence

One of the most significant problems when trying to figure out how to get two systems to talk to each other is sorting out what dependencies, assumptions, and standards to use. For example, we assume that we will be using TCP/IP and the other core technologies of the Internet, but we may not (for example) be comfortable assuming that our partners are willing to standardize on Java or .NET technologies. Instead of declaring required technologies by fiat, our first instinct is to wait and see what standards get locked down.

Preferably, the standards we choose have several solid implementations and have been in use for some time. This allows us to understand more of the pros and cons of any particular technology. HTML, for example, has been in use for some time, but different web browsers can have wildly different interpretations of a given HTML document. Many of the same problems you see with HTML can be seen with web services; for example, consider the seemingly simple questions of style and perspective reflected in the differences between the HTML pages shown in Examples 1-1 and 1-2 (both display the same text on screen).

Example 1-1. Simple HTML

```
<HTML>
    <HEAD>
    </HEAD>
    <BODY>
        <P ALIGN="CENTER"><B>This is my text!</B></P>
    </BODY>
</HTML>
```

Example 1-1 shows a very human-readable (yet not particularly elegant or sophisticated) version of an HTML page. Example 1-2 shows a page without any extraneous formatting or whitespace, with proper markers and the (admittedly gratuitous) use of CSS.

Example 1-2. Complex HTML

```
<!DOCTYPE HTML PUBLIC "-//W3C//DTD HTML 4.01 Transitional//EN"
"http://www.w3.org/TR/html4/loose.dtd"><html><head>
<meta http-equiv="Content-Type" content="text/html; charset=iso-8859-1">
<style type="text/css"><!-- P { font-style: normal; font-weight: bold;
    text-align: center; } --></style></head>
<body><p>This is my text! </p></body></html>
```

Sometimes differences are merely a matter of style and not substance. For example, consider the differences in method naming standards between Java and Microsoft C/C++. Java developers typically prefer relatively verbose naming, with a strong object-as-noun, method-as-verb nomenclature, heavily influenced by the patterns put forth by the JavaBeans specification that you'll find at:

http://java.sun.com/docs/codeconv/html/CodeConvTOC.doc.html

Microsoft developers are more likely to use Hungarian notation, which as even Microsoft notes, "make the variable names look a bit as though they're written in some non-English language"; see the following for more information:

http://msdn.microsoft.com/library/en-us/dnvsgen/html/HungaNotat.asp

However,.NET is phasing this out; see the following:

*http://msdn.microsoft.com/library/default.asp?url=/library/en-us/cpgenref/html/
cpconNaming-Guidelines.asp*

While style issues are relevant when you talk about web services—as you'll see, a perfectly usable set of web service interfaces provided by a vendor can still feel very awkward if the interfaces are based on another style and mental model—the important thing is that services can still be accessed in a reliable, predictable manner. The goal when using web services is to get away from wildly undefined and fragile processes (such as scraping HTML) and instead move toward refined, manageable systems.

Planning for Interdependence

The pundits, purveyors, and snake oil salesmen of web services describe a world in which nearly every process is handled seamlessly by a variety of different web service technologies and options. Automated agents, interconnected by wired and wireless technologies, will use web services to solve global economic crises, find you the best deal on toasters, and restock your refrigerator with fresh milk before you've even noticed that the expiration date has passed.

This deeply interconnected world assumes that the underlying web services work very well. In particular, such broad-reaching automation leads to basic questions about responsibilities. For example, let's say that an error leads to your refrigerator ordering 500 gallons of milk—or none at all. Where did the problem occur? This issue affects you both as a user and provider of web services.

To manage questions of reliability, you must determine what sort of uptime you provide (or demand) for your web services. How do you characterize the performance and security restrictions? What are the implications of a service failure?

It can be helpful to build a brief worksheet when working with web services that can be used as a check list. It can include:

* Number of web service methods exposed or used
* Frequency of access allowed (e.g., one method call per second at most for methods a( ), b( ), c( ), and one call of method d( ) per minute)
* Expected performance of specific methods
* Time expected to restore service (e.g., if there is a failure, how long until it's fixed?)
* Bandwidth and latency expectations
* Scheduled downtime
* Data management and backup responsibility
* Logging
* Security auditing

Here are some questions to ask yourself:

* What are your internal plans for migration if the service fails?
* What is the involvement of your legal representation in drafting or agreeing to your service agreement?
* What tools or systems will you use to monitor your services? (If you promise to deliver or receive a given level of service, how will you really know?)
* What is the expected level of tech support access? How are users expected to contact support? How long until a response is sent?

- How will minor bug fixes and upgrades be handled? Will users of the web services be able to test their application against a test server before the changes are pushed to the production system?
- How often will new functionality be added? What is the procedure for migrating web service users to new systems?
- How long will session data be preserved? (In other words, if I begin a transaction, how long does the remote system maintain that state data before expiring it?)
- What are the remedies (refunds or credits) if service fails?

Notice that there is no mention of the programming language used, the application server, the database, the server hardware—all critical to the internal development conversation, but (in theory, at least) not part of the overall web services conversation between two different organizations.

Because of the complexities of interdependence, when you're working with web services, you need at least a basic understanding of the underlying networking principles, which are discussed in the next chapter.

CHAPTER 2

Foundations of Web Services

This chapter takes a high-level look at the technical underpinnings of web services. It's important to understand these concepts and technologies when trying to debug problems, which in turn, can help you understand the conceptual relationship between different aspects of web services.

Basic Networking

A computer network is essentially nothing more than the notion of two or more independent computers "connected" to each other in some fashion. This, liberally applied, can be used to describe two fax machines, two digital phones, a few personal computers (and perhaps a TiVo), or, more generally, a local area network, a wide area network, or even the Internet itself.

There's a tremendous amount of physical infrastructure behind establishing these connections. Most of us are familiar with both physical and wireless networks (in particular, the 10/100/1000Base-T physical and various 802.11 wireless technologies). Consider the wireless router connected to the switch, connected to the DSL modem, connected to the service provider's network, and then the various connections that lead to (for example) the local Amazon.com server. It's hard to say which is more amazing—that a packet ever gets to the destination or that a response finds its way back.

Just sorting out the basic components of a network can be a very conceptually difficult area, so let's turn to the time honored standby, the International Standard Organization's Open System Interconnect (OSI) model (see Table 2-1). Perhaps one of the best diagrams for discussing networking fundamentals, the OSI reference model is a conceptual, seven-tiered "stack" showing the relationship between the different components of a network.

Table 2-1. ISO's OSI stack

Layer	Example(s)
Physical layer	RJ-45 connectors, CAT5
Data Link layer	Ethernet (IEEE 802.2)
Network layer	IP, IPX
Transport layer	TCP, UDP
Session layer	Socket connections
Presentation layer	Byte ordering
Application layer	HTTP, FTP, SMTP, POP3, IMAP, etc.

The OSI model is regarded as a theoretical tool, not a practical system for working with (or building) a network, but it's worth noting for purposes of understanding the complexity of the underlying system. It's beyond the scope of this text to cover this model in detail, but when working with web services, it's more or less assumed that all the layers beneath the application layer "just work." When things go wrong, it can be useful to walk through the model to understand exactly where things are going awry.

 There are numerous excellent descriptions of lower-level networking topics. For a comprehensive description of various network protocols, I enjoyed Matthew Naugle's *Network Protocol Handbook* (McGraw-Hill). It's a dated but very detailed look at networking fundamentals as expressed by a variety of networking approaches (many of which are now mostly historical).

Note that the application layer as described by the OSI isn't the same thing as an application. Applications, be they servers or desktop clients, generally rely on the underlying application layer (sometimes referred to as a protocol) for the actual communication.

A uniform resource identifier (URI), as shown in Figure 2-1, contains the minimum information an application needs to access information on the Internet. The port is often assumed for certain protocols (e.g., port 80 is the default for HTTP). Given a URI, most system libraries allow for access to network resources as input and output streams of bytes.

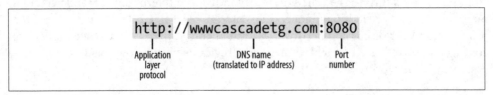

Figure 2-1. Uniform resource identifier

Libraries sometimes provide application developers with a more friendly view of data transmitted over a network. For example, the Java servlet APIs provide programmatic access to HTTP requests, abstracting away the lower level details of the data transfer. These libraries allow a developer to avoid writing custom code for every network connection, instead focusing on the portion of the network transfer relevant to the application.

Streams of Bytes

Using the Apache Axis TCPMonitor application, we can monitor the raw bytes exchanged when the O'Reilly web site is accessed by a web browser (see Figure 2-2). The top pane shows the various connection data, the middle pane shows the data sent to the O'Reilly web server, and the bottom pane shows the data returned (you can see the various HTTP headers and the start of the actual HTML). For more information on the Apache Axis TCPMonitor application, see *http://ws.apache.org/axis/java/user-guide.html*.

```
Keep-Alive: timeout=15, max=500
Connection: Keep-Alive

<!DOCTYPE HTML PUBLIC "-//W3C//DTD HTML 4.01 Transitional//E
<html xmlns="http://www.w3.org/1999/xhtml" lang="en-US" xml:
<head>
<title>www.oreilly.com -- Welcome to O'Reilly &amp; Associat
<meta name="keywords" content="O'Reilly, oreilly, computer b
technical books, UNIX, unix, Perl, Java, Linux, Internet, Wel
<meta name="description" content="O'Reilly is a leader in te
<script language="JavaScript" type="text/javascript" src="ht
```

Figure 2-2. Raw bytes from accessing oreilly.com

In the remainder of this book, we'll focus on the application layer and code built on it. Instead of accessing raw bytes, we'll use libraries that digest these network streams and provide additional services.

Viewing the textual structure seen in the sent and returned bytes shown in Figure 2-2, it's easy to imagine building your own server or client to send and receive this sort of data. By establishing common protocols for communication, it's possible to decouple the server and client applications, allowing for incremental replacement of either the server or the client over time. Using HTTP as an example, it's possible to upgrade your browser without upgrading every server on the Internet (and vice versa). This separation is a critical aspect of web services.

Sometimes, standards for interaction become confusing as protocols and systems are chained together. For example, SOAP, formerly known as Simple Object Access Protocol,* relies on HTTP, the Hypertext Transfer Protocol, to exchange data. Alternatively, SOAP can send data via SMTP, the Simple Mail Transport Protocol. It's easy to see how the already complex OSI reference model can begin to feel a bit simplistic when a SOAP service is layered on top of HTTP, which might then in turn be layered on top of SSL for encryption.

A Multitude of Standards

The various different standards, while potentially helpful for developers, also can lead to confusion. For example, visiting the *http://www.xml.com/* web site, you see the following topics listed as "Essentials":

- What is XML?
- What is XSLT?
- What is XSL-FO?
- What is XLink?
- What is XML Schema?
- What is XQuery?
- What is RDF?
- What is RSS?
- What are Topic Maps?
- What are Web Services?
- What are XForms?

Admittedly, many of these are germane primarily to XML manipulation, not web services per se, but this is representative of the profusion of XML/web service "standards" and specifications. There are literally dozens of competing documents purporting to be standards for a variety of web service related topics, including security, business processes, and many more.

Most of these standards are designed to allow for libraries and tools that help developers to avoid "getting dirty" by messing around with the underlying byte streams, or to avoid vendor lock-in. The challenge is to determine which standards are relevant for a given situation.

The complexities of the network are typically reduced for the application programmer into streams of bytes. Unfortunately, a stream of bytes delivered over the

---

* SOAP is officially no longer an acronym for anything.

network isn't predictable or reliable, and so any networked application must still deal with network vagaries.

Network Vagaries

At the core, network vagaries boil down to three main points:

- *Latency*, or the delay until the first bit arrives
- *Bandwidth*, or the total bits sent over a period of time
- *Reliability*, or the notion that bits sent are bits received

As you can see in Table 2-2, different physical connections have different characteristics. For example, a burned and priority-mailed DVD, while featuring terrible latency, is a comparatively high-bandwidth solution. The same is true for protocols: if you compare HTTP and SMTP (two of the underlying transports possible for SOAP), SMTP offers superior reliability but greater latency than HTTP.

Table 2-2. Comparing different physical network connections

	Latency	Bandwidth	Reliability
Dial-up	Poor	Poor	Moderate
DSL/cable	Good	Good	Good
Cell phone PDA	Poor	Poor	Poor
802.11x laptop	Good	Moderate	Moderate
Colocated server	Excellent	Excellent	Excellent
Handwritten letter	Poor	Poor	Excellent
A file copied to a floppy	Poor	Poor	Excellent
A burned and priority-mailed DVD	Terrible	Excellent	Excellent

As developers, we tend to make assumptions about networks that simply aren't correct—for instance, about the nature of the client's needs or capabilities or that the network is even available at all (a form of reliability). The following quote is from "The Eight Fallacies of Distributed Computing," by Peter Deutsch, which can be found at *http://today.java.net/jag/Fallacies.html*:

> Essentially everyone, when they first build a distributed application, makes the following eight assumptions. All prove to be false in the long run and all cause big trouble and painful learning experiences.
>
> > The network is reliable
> > Latency is zero
> > Bandwidth is infinite
> > The network is secure
> > Topology doesn't change
> > There is one administrator
> > Transport cost is zero
> > The network is homogeneous

This book assumes that you understand how your underlying network works (and how to secure your network using, for example, firewalls). If you wish to provide web services, you may need to punch a hole through your firewall or set up port forwarding to ensure that the IP address exposed to the Internet is forwarded to the particular machine on the local network providing the service.

If your application is going to principally use HTTP-based web services, you probably don't need to worry about the network configuration (assuming you can successfully browse the Internet). Many web services are assigned the standard HTTP port (80), but some services use alternate ports (e.g., 8080). If you have trouble connecting to a web service, you should check to make sure that the port is not blocked by a firewall.

Throughout this book, we'll assume a simple network, running on a 192.168.1.x subnet. The network is connected to the to the Internet by a port-forwarded firewall/ router connected to a DSL line. This is likely simpler than the production network you'll be using, but it will work for our purposes.

HTTP

HTTP requests are just that—an incoming request from a client (typically a web browser) to a server for a specific document. It's worth looking at this a bit closer. Let's start by looking at the two main methods for retrieving a document via HTTP, GET and POST.

GET

Generally speaking, a GET is a simple request for a page with some parameters sent in a specific format. Examine the request shown Example 2-1, as you might type into the address field of your browser.

Example 2-1. HTTP GET request URI

```
http://localhost:1234/example.jsp?page=12&format=simple
```

Looking at the HTTP GET request, notice that the request contains two parameters: page and format. When the web application gets this request, it may examine these parameters and return different results based on the values of these parameters. Example 2-2 shows the actual text sent to the web server.

Example 2-2. Bytes sent for a HTTP GET request

```
GET /example.jsp?page=12&format=simple HTTP/1.1
Host: cascadetg.com
User-Agent: Mozilla/5.0 (Windows; U; Windows NT 5.1; en-US; rv:1.5) Gecko/20031007
Firebird/0.7
```

Example 2-2. Bytes sent for a HTTP GET request (continued)

```
Accept: text/xml,application/xml,application/xhtml+xml,text/html;q=0.9,text/plain;q=0.
8,video/x-mng,image/png,image/jpeg,image/gif;q=0.2,*/*;q=0.1
Accept-Language: en-us,en;q=0.5
Accept-Encoding: gzip,deflate
Accept-Charset: ISO-8859-1,utf-8;q=0.7,*;q=0.7
Keep-Alive: 300
Connection: keep-alive
Cookie: CP=null*
```

In many ways, it can help to think of a page request as a very simple execution of a command-line program or even a just a function being called. Conceptually, this is how a servlet works at the most primitive level: a stream of bytes from the client is passed in, and a stream of bytes is then sent back.

POST

A POST is conceptually similar to a GET but with slightly different formatting. A POST is commonly used to handle a form submission, with more complex data sent to the server than a GET. Example 2-3 shows a simple HTML form.

Example 2-3. HTML form

```html
<!DOCTYPE HTML PUBLIC "-//W3C//DTD HTML 4.01 Transitional//EN"
"http://www.w3.org/TR/html4/loose.dtd">
<html>
<head>
<title>Simple Form</title>
<meta http-equiv="Content-Type" content="text/html; charset=iso-8859-1">
</head>
<body>
<form action="http://localhost:1234/" method="post"
    enctype="multipart/form-data" name="simpleForm" id="simpleForm">
  <p>Text  Field <input type="text" name="textfield"></p>
  <p>File to upload <input type="file" name="file"></p>
  <p><input type="submit" name="Submit" value="Submit">
  </p>
</form>
</body>
</html>
```

You'll notice the emphasis on the form tags in the example. These input elements generate user interface elements in the web browser. When the user clicks on the Submit button, as shown in Figure 2-3, the web browser examines these user interface elements and returns the appropriate data to the web server.

An example of the data sent to the server is shown in Example 2-4. You'll notice that the values of the text field and the Submit button are sent as part of this text.

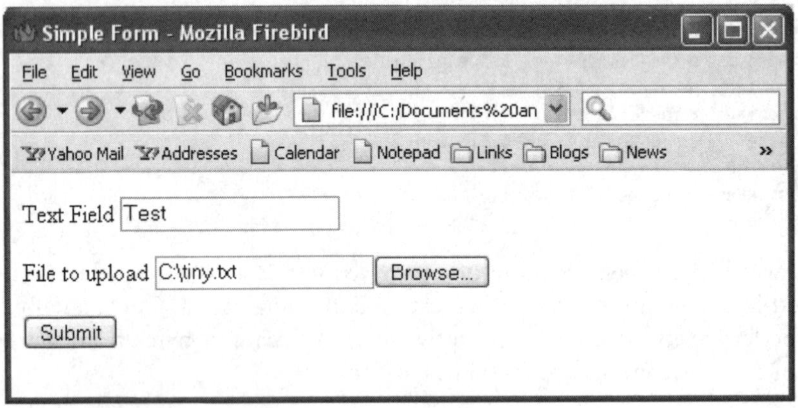

Figure 2-3. A simple HTML form

Example 2-4. Bytes sent for an HTTP POST request

```
POST / HTTP/1.1
Host: cascadetg.com
User-Agent: Mozilla/5.0 (Windows; U; Windows NT 5.1; en-US; rv:1.5) Gecko/20031007
Firebird/0.7
Accept: text/xml,application/xml,application/xhtml+xml,text/html;q=0.9,text/plain;q=0.
8,video/x-mng,image/png,image/jpeg,image/gif;q=0.2,*/*;q=0.1
Accept-Language: en-us,en;q=0.5
Accept-Encoding: gzip,deflate
Accept-Charset: ISO-8859-1,utf-8;q=0.7,*;q=0.7
Keep-Alive: 300
Connection: keep-alive
Cookie: CP=null*
Content-Type: multipart/form-data; boundary=---------------------------41184676334
Content-Length: 438

---------------------------41184676334
Content-Disposition: form-data; name="textfield"

Test
---------------------------41184676334
Content-Disposition: form-data; name="file"; filename="tiny.txt"
Content-Type: text/plain

A small text file.

Nothing to see here.  Move along.

---------------------------41184676334
Content-Disposition: form-data; name="Submit"

Submit
---------------------------41184676334--
```

Note that the file is encoded and sent along with the rest of the content in this request (using MIME-based encoding). This demonstrates how a simple stream of bytes can contain complex information, including form data and even files. Most of the standard Internet protocols, such as HTTP, NNTP (used in Usenet newsgroups), SMTP, POP, and FTP are based on similar (more or less) human-readable formats. In many ways, these textual formats aren't particularly efficient, but they are easy to understand and debug. The main difference between "classic" Internet protocols, such as HTTP and NNTP, and web service protocols (such as SOAP) is the reliance on XML for presenting and parsing the bytes.

Potential of Bytes

Once you start thinking of the Internet and networking as readable (and possibly mutable) streams of bytes, many interesting ideas become apparent. For example, certain products read and then pass along streams of bytes. A stream might alter a web page to block pornography or generate reports on the information being sent. Another obvious example is a server application that goes out on the Internet, automatically downloads web pages, searches for links and other information, and then builds a searchable index (such as Google.com and other Internet search engines).

As discussed in Chapter 1, it turns out one popular idea is to read the contents of other web pages, parse the HTML, and then generate your own "new" page featuring that content. Aside from being illegal and extremely rude, it's incredibly inefficient. You may only be interested in one or two thousand bytes in that response, and yet Amazon is sending you a hundred times that much data (HTML formatting, information about other products, etc.). It's much more efficient to directly call another server with a request, and just receive the data you're looking for—in other words, a remote procedure call.

From HTTP to RPC

Remote procedure calls, or RPC, have been around for a long time. The concept is simple: let's say you have a function along the lines of the following:

```
int adjustBankAccount(long account, float adjustment);
```

Expressed in a more object-oriented syntax, you might have something more along the lines of this:

```
BankAccount.adjust(Money amount);
```

Now, these methods are pretty easy to understand and work with as part of a program compiled and running on a single machine. An RPC is, in theory, the same thing; however, instead you're making the method call code on another machine. So, consider this code:

```
// Local code
Money adjustment = new Money(1.50);
```

```
// Remote code
myBankAccount.adjust(adjustment);
```

The reference to `myBankAccount.adjust( )` is converted by the underlying RPC framework into a request made to the bank server, with all the underlying argument data type, networking, and error-handling code taken care of for you. In theory, you're working with code running on another system just as easily as you work with local code!

Leaky RPC Plumbing

The reality, unfortunately, tends to be a bit more complicated. It's what you call a *leaky abstraction*: the idea that a method call on a local system is the same as a method call on a remote system hides a lot of important details. The most basic are the issues of latency, reliability, and bandwidth (as discussed earlier in this chapter). Other issues include security and availability. Perhaps most significantly, different programming languages and operating systems have wildly different ideas about such matters as method calls, type information, error handling, and more. This becomes an extremely political issue because pretty much everyone seems to recognize that if a particular standard for remote procedure calls becomes dominant, all other environments risk withering (much as network standards competitive with TCP/IP continue to fade).

Early attempts at these distributed systems included CORBA, DCOM, Java RMI, and a host of others. These attempts encountered tremendous difficulty establishing themselves as standards because they weren't compatible with nonproprietary environments (Java RMI and DCOM) or they were overwhelmingly complex (DSOM* and CORBA). Interestingly, all these attempts encoded their data in a binary format, offering potentially high performance but at a significant cost: they were uniformly difficult to understand, debug, and implement.

RPC Meets the Internet

As the Internet came to the fore and XML became popular, many people noticed that it was easy to use an HTTP GET or POST to retrieve an XML document. Pretty much everyone, regardless of programming language or environment, had some sort of wrapper library to easily access the data returned by an HTTP GET, and there was a profusion of XML parsers. Instead of using a cumbersome build process to generate a host of files to access proprietary binary data, people realized that they could build an RPC system using simple, existing technologies and standards.

---

* *http://www.webopedia.com/TERM/D/DSOM.html*

Arguably the first true Internet web service framework (and still one of the most simple and easy to use) is XML-RPC (*http://www.xmlrpc.com/*). It's a pretty terse specification, but if you just need to get a small amount of information over the wire, it's hard to think of a much easier mechanism. Notably, a variety of libraries exist in a variety of programming languages, allowing different systems to easily share data using XML-RPC.

Evolving to SOAP

Unfortunately, XML-RPC suffered from a number of problems due to the lack of sufficiently detailed specification. Certain limitations (e.g., the inability to specify a language encoding for strings other than English ASCII) meant that the specification was bound to fracture as it tried to gain wide adoption.

Despite these limitations, XML-RPC served as a powerful precursor to its eventual replacement, SOAP. It showed that it was possible to define a very simple specification for performing RPC via the Internet, using XML as the packaging.

SOAP

The Simple Object Access Protocol is perhaps one of the worst names ever chosen for a technology. While it is (in theory) simple, you often get the impression that vendors are doing everything they can to make it as complex as possible. The term "object" in SOAP would seem to imply some connection to object-oriented development, but instead SOAP is almost totally procedural in nature. Finally, "protocol" might convey some sense that it's a replacement or upgrade to HTTP or SMTP, but instead SOAP relies on these protocols to actually handle data transfer. SOAP is effectively XML-RPC's bigger, more sophisticated younger brother. The specification, now at Version 1.2, is maintained by the W3C XML Protocol Working Group at *http://www.w3.org/2000/xp/Group/*.

Simply put, SOAP provides rules for handling remote procedure calls using XML as the wrapping protocol (called an *envelope*). This reliance on XML makes it easier to implement SOAP infrastructure. Most programming languages now offer SOAP support, making working with SOAP a relatively familiar, XML-parsing-free experience.

To see how to work with SOAP as an RPC system, let's look at the snippet of code shown in Example 2-5 (from the Apache Axis project).

Example 2-5. Accessing SOAP from Java

```
package samples.userguide.example1;

import org.apache.axis.client.Call;
import org.apache.axis.client.Service;
```

Example 2-5. Accessing SOAP from Java (continued)

```java
import javax.xml.namespace.QName;

public class TestClient
{
    public static void main(String [] args) {
        try {
            Service service = new Service( );
            Call call = (Call) service.createCall( );

            call.setTargetEndpointAddress(new java.net.URL(
             "http://nagoya.apache.org:5049/axis/services/echo"));
            call.setOperationName(
             new QName("http://soapinterop.org/", "echoString"));

            String ret = (String)call.invoke(new Object[]{"Hello!"});

            System.out.println("Sent 'Hello!', got '" + ret + "'");
        } catch (Exception e) {
            System.err.println(e.toString( ));
        }
    }
}
```

There is no reference in Example 2-5 to XML. Interestingly, a popular use of SOAP is to transmit XML data. This means that you are, in effect, wrapping an XML document inside another XML document, then using HTTP or SMTP to move data around. Fortunately, you don't actually have to worry about this; the SOAP libraries take care of the details of these rather confusing tasks for you.

Giving SOAP a REST?

Instead of SOAP, you can use a methodology called Representational State Transfer (REST). In many ways, REST is a return to the simpler XML-RPC concept, because it lets you interchange XML documents using standard HTTP concepts. That said, REST is an architectural style without a concrete specification; as a result, using REST is a lot closer to opening up a stream of bytes.

For more information on REST, consult *http://conveyor.com/RESTwiki/moin.cgi*.

As you can imagine, it is quite convenient when working with SOAP to use various developer tools to more seamlessly integrate remote services. This led to the emergence of another technology, WSDL.

Web Services Definition Language

The Web Services Definition Language, or WSDL, is a specification for describing the methods and data types provided by a SOAP interface. This sort of metadata is very useful when trying to build tools that support SOAP, much the same way that the JavaBeans specification provides support for an IDE to graphically wire together a visual application.

To understand the distinction between the metadata and the actual object, consider the programmatic interfaces you use when building your application. For example, C developers use header files to share the functions exposed by their library. The headers are analogous to WSDL, whereas the linked methods are analogous to a SOAP message or payload.

It's true that you don't need WSDL to access a SOAP service, but it can be slow-going work without it. Instead, it's often easier to feed a vendor-provided WSDL to your tools and have them build language-specific bindings. For example, a developer using C# tools can easily work with a Java-based server if given an appropriate WSDL file. We won't be spending a lot of time worrying about how to generate WSDL files, because most environments provide mechanisms for automatically generating WSDL from the services you expose. We will, however, be using WSDL presented by other vendors to reduce the drudgery of building our applications.

As we walk through the progression from basic networking, HTTP, and then on to SOAP and WSDL as RPC mechanisms, it would seem only logical that most of the modern web services offered today are built using SOAP and WSDL. Instead, as you'll see, many web services are available as raw XML delivered via HTTP (such as eBay or FedEx) or even just a stream of specially formatted text (such as CDDB1, described in Chapter 9).

The next chapter looks at setting up our development environment and then get started actually building web service-based applications.

CHAPTER 3

Development Platform

This chapter looks at the tools and systems used to build applications throughout the rest of the book. I'm assuming that you have some basic familiarity with building Java applications already. You should be familiar with basic object-oriented development, know how to add libraries to your class path,* understand TCP/IP and basic networking, and be familiar with basic JSP-based web application development. You don't need to be familiar with Enterprise JavaBeans™ (EJB) or other J2EE technologies, such as Java Message Service (JMS).

The sample applications demonstrate the easiest mechanisms for accessing web services. This book isn't concerned with the persistence layer of the application. It's up to you to decide the best mechanism for saving data. You may want to store your data on the filesystem or in a relational database, using any of a variety of APIs such as JDBC or Java Data Objects (JDO).

We will use Java exclusively (specifically, all examples are built and tested on Windows XP Professional, Java Version 1.4.2_03). If you don't already have Java 1.4.2 or later installed, please visit *http://java.sun.com/*, and download and install the J2SE 1.4 SDK. You may be offered the opportunity to download the NetBeans integrated development environment (IDE) bundled with the SDK; if you don't already have a Java development environment, this is an excellent choice (the free, open source Eclipse, *http://www.eclipse.org/*, is another excellent, free Java IDE).

Tools and Projects Used

There are several projects and tools that are used extensively throughout the book. You should take the time to get each one set up and operating on your machine, so

---

* Per the official Java documentation, class path (with a space) refers to the concept of a class path, whereas classpath (or CLASSPATH) refers to either a specific instance or the system environment variable. This is an important distinction because a web server or Java application may (or may not) respect other class path declarations (such as a CLASSPATH environment variable).

you can focus on writing code in the later chapters, rather than fool with configuration files.

Apache Jakarta Tomcat

Apache Jakarta Tomcat is a popular, free, open source application server. It serves as the reference implementation of the Java Servlet and JavaServer Pages specifications. You can download Tomcat at *http://jakarta.apache.org/tomcat/*.

This book was written using Tomcat 5.0.18. If you run Windows, you can download and run a standard Windows installer that will install the software. On Windows, I recommend installing the software into the *C:\Tomcat5* directory instead of the default *C:\Program Files\Apache Software Foundation\Tomcat 5.0\common\lib* directory, as certain software can have problems with spaces in the directory path. On other platforms (such as Mac OS X and Unix-based system), you should download the *.tar, .gz,* or *.zip* version.

> If you see errors when attempting to compile JSP pages while running Tomcat 5.0, you may need to copy the *tools.jar* file (containing the javac compiler) into your Tomcat installation. If you installed the Java 1.4.2_03 with the bundled NetBeans in the default directory on Windows, you can find *tools.jar* file at *C:\Program Files\j2sdk_nb\j2sdk1.4.2\lib\tools.jar*. Copy this *tools.jar* file to *C:\Program Files\Apache Software Foundation\Tomcat 5.0\common\lib* and restart Tomcat.

Tomcat uses several directories for managing the class path; you should be familiar with the different directories when building your own web applications. For more information on where to place your classes, see *http://jakarta.apache.org/tomcat/tomcat-5.0-doc/class-loader-howto.html*.

Tomcat is by no means the only Java application server suitable for web services; virtually every major technology vendor (with the exception of Microsoft) offers a Java-based application server, including Sun Microsystems, IBM, BEA, and Macromedia. There are also a variety of other open source application servers, including JBoss (*http://www.jboss.org/*) and Enhydra (*http://www.enhydra.org/*). As long as the server supports Servlet 2.3/JSP 1.2 or later, you should expect to be able to run the examples provided in this text.

Apache XML-RPC

In some of the examples in this book, we use Apache Axis's older, less complex brother, XML-RPC (*http://www.xml-rpc.com/*). You can download the Apache implementation of XML-RPC at *http://ws.apache.org/xmlrpc/* (Version 1.2b-1 was used in this text). The XML-RPC distribution is shown in Figure 3-1.

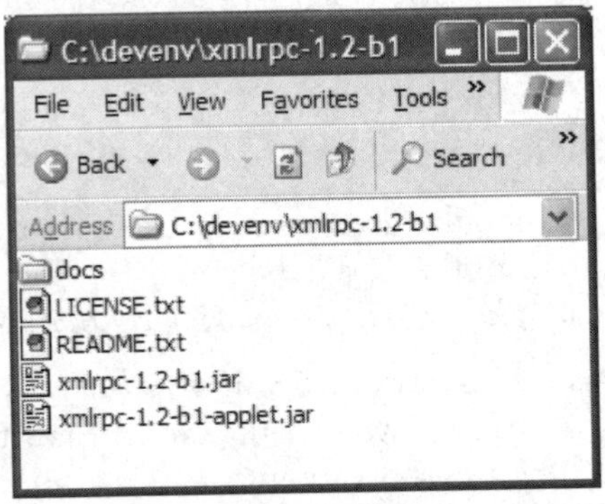

Figure 3-1. Apache XML-RPC installation layout

Notice in the figure that there is just a single XML-RPC JAR file: you must add this JAR to your class path.

Apache Axis

Apache Axis is the latest iteration of the Apache SOAP web service toolkit, providing support for both SOAP and WSDL. You can use Axis to create your own web services or to act as a client for other web services.

You can download Axis at *http://ws.apache.org/axis/*. This book uses Axis 1.1, the latest stable release as of this writing. The download, *axis-1_1.tar.gz* or *axis-1_1.zip*, should be decompressed into an easily accessible, permanent location. The directories included in the Axis 1.1 distribution are shown in Figure 3-2.

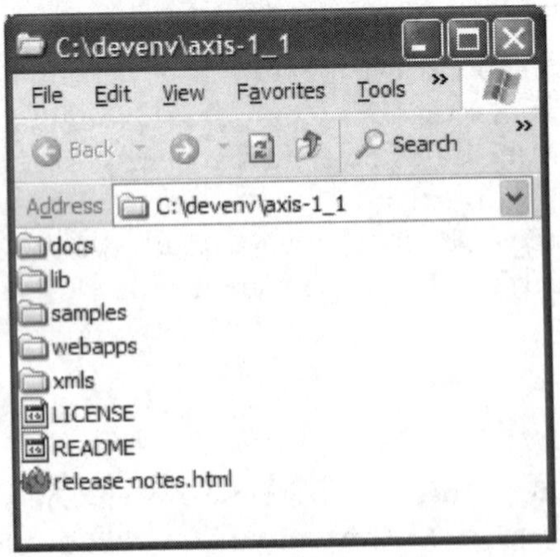

Figure 3-2. Axis 1.1 installation directory

The Axis 1.1 *lib* directory contains several JAR files needed by Axis (in addition to the core library, *axis.jar*). Keep in mind that there are two main uses of Axis: first, as a set of libraries that provide services for client and server web applications, and second, as a tool to generate Java bindings from a WSDL file. Therefore, you will likely want to add the various JAR files in the Axis *lib* directory to your application class path, and also retain a copy for use with generating the WSDL bindings. I'll demonstrate creating and using a SOAP web service later in this chapter.

There are a variety of other toolkits available for both consuming and producing SOAP- and WSDL-based services. In particular, many commercial application servers offer proprietary toolkits. That said, Apache Axis can be dropped into most popular Java application servers and is listed as a supported toolkit by all the vendors offering SOAP web services in this book. In the event that you need to change application server vendors, it's much easier to migrate Axis-based applications to other systems than to migrate applications based on a proprietary toolkit.

Test Drive

The primary focus of this book is not on creating your own web services—there are numerous other texts that describe how to do this (including several from O'Reilly)—but on using existing web services in productive and useful ways. However, it is helpful to understand how to create a web service because it illustrates some of the complexities when consuming a web service. Here, we will create both a client and a server for a simple "Hello World" web service using Tomcat and Axis. In addition to the learning value, this exercise tests out the tools mentioned, ensuring you're ready for the more complex examples in the rest of the book.

First, copy the contents of the *axis-1_1\webapps\axis* directory to your Tomcat *webapps* directory, as shown in Figure 3-3.

After copying the files, launch Tomcat. After Tomcat launches, point your browser at *http://localhost:8080/axis/*. You should see the status message shown in Figure 3-4.

Clicking the link to "Validate" your installation, you will find that you are missing three needed components, *activation.jar*, *mail.jar*, and *xmlsec.jar*.

The first, *activation.jar*, is required to get Axis off the launchpad. The second, *mail.jar*, is required for examples later in this book that use the SMTP. Links to these libraries (available from Sun Microsystems) are displayed directly in the error message.

 As of this writing, the latest versions of the required components are Java Activation Framework 1.0.2 and JavaMail 1.3.1.

These two libraries are used by many web applications; you are best off placing them in the Tomcat *shared/lib* directory, as shown in Figure 3-5.

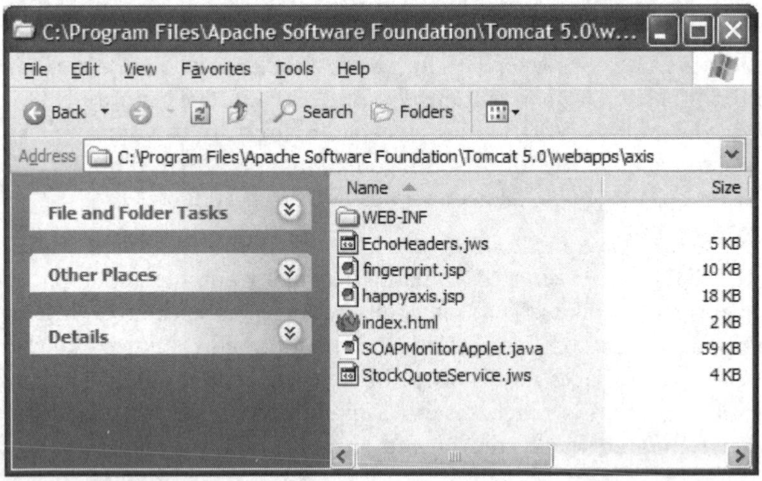

Figure 3-3. Copying the Axis sample web application

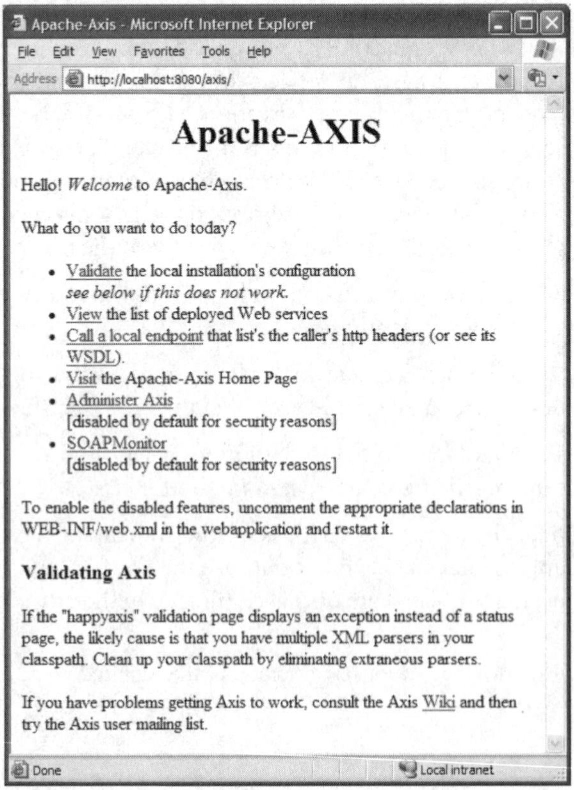

Figure 3-4. Axis opening page

Figure 3-5. Installing the required Axis libraries

You must restart Tomcat to load the libraries. After restarting, reload the URL, *http://localhost:8080/axis/happyaxis.jsp*, to verify the needed libraries are now successfully loaded (as shown in Figure 3-6).

The third optional library, *xmlsec.jar* (XML Security), digitally signs XML documents—a potentially useful capability but (sadly) one that is not supported by any of the web service offerings covered in this text.

Our First SOAP Server

Let's create a simple SOAP-based web service using Axis.

Axis supports a method of web services generation similar to the way you create a web page using a JSP: an ordinary Java source file, when given the *.jws* extension and placed in an Axis-enabled web application, is automatically converted into a Java web service (hence the *.jws* extension).

Create a file called *CurrentDate.jws* in the Axis *webapp* directory. The results should be as shown in Figure 3-7.

The contents of *CurrentDate.jws* are shown in Example 3-1. As you can see, a *.jws* file is essentially an ordinary Java source file. Axis automatically compiles and wraps this file as a web service when requested by an appropriate client (such as a web browser or a SOAP client). The dynamic compilation process is similar to that provided by JSP; you can modify the JWS file, switch to your browser, hit refresh, and the file is automatically recompiled and made available as a web service—no need for manual compilation or a complex deployment process.

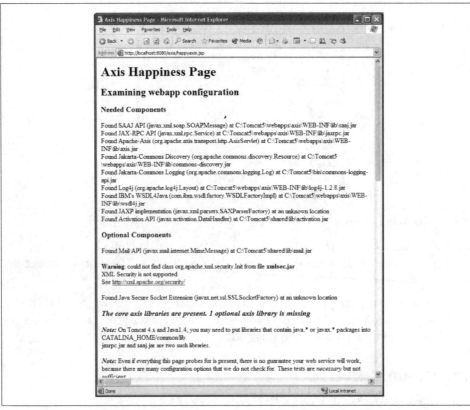

Figure 3-6. Axis validation page

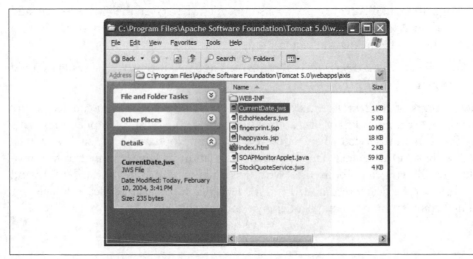

Figure 3-7. Creating CurrentDate.jws

Example 3-1. Current date web service

```java
public class CurrentDate
{
    public String now()
    {
        return new java.util.Date().toString();
    }

    public int add(int a, int b)
    {
        return a + b;
    }
}
```

Public classes and methods in *.jws* files wrapped and exposed by Axis are automatically made available to inquiring web services. Pointing our web browser at *http://localhost:8080/axis/CurrentDate.jws*, notice that Axis is aware of the *.jws* file at this location, as shown in Figure 3-8.

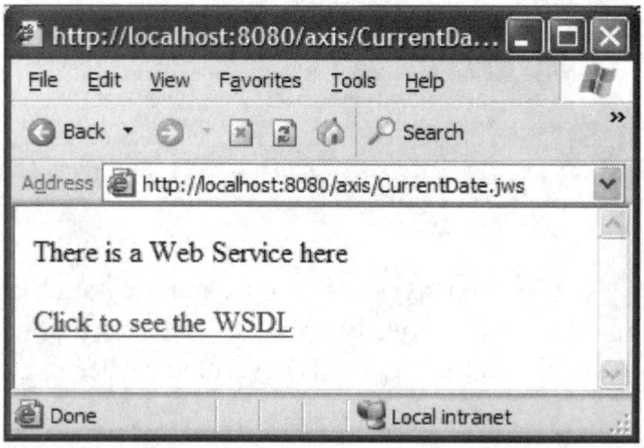

Figure 3-8. Viewing CurrentDate.jws with a browser

The *.jws* file isn't actually compiled until you request either the service or the WSDL file. Compilation errors are reported in the web browser, similar to JSP. Clicking on the link for the WSDL shows the automatically generated WSDL file, as seen in Figure 3-9.

The automatically generated WSDL file shows that the *CurrentDate.jws* has been compiled and is now available for use by clients.

Dynamic SOAP Client

By a *dynamic* SOAP client, I mean that the information about the web service is constructed at runtime, as opposed to being precompiled. This runtime construction of a web service request allows for very rapid development when initially connecting to

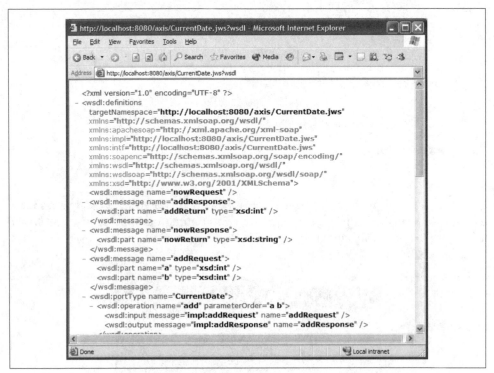

Figure 3-9. Viewing CurrentDate.jws WSDL

a web service: simply cut and paste the relevant elements, such as the URL and the SOAP method names into your code. Example 3-2 shows a simple dynamic SOAP example, which accesses the SOAP Server as described earlier.

Example 3-2. Dynamic SOAP client

```
package com.cascadetg.ch03;

// axis.jar
import org.apache.axis.client.Call;
import org.apache.axis.client.Service;

// jaxrpc.jar
import javax.xml.namespace.QName;

public class DynamicCurrentDateClient
{
    public static void main(String[] args)
    {
        try
        {
```

Example 3-2. Dynamic SOAP client (continued)

```
        // Create a Axis client
        Service service = new Service();

        // Create a method call object
        Call call = (Call)service.createCall();

        // Point to the web service
        call.setTargetEndpointAddress(
            new java.net.URL(
                "http://localhost:8080/axis/CurrentDate.jws"));

        // First, let's call the now method
        call.setOperationName(new QName("now"));

        System.out.print(
            "According to the web service, it is now ");
        System.out.println((String)call.invoke(new Object[0]));

        // Let's reuse the same method object, but this time,
        // call the add method
        call.setOperationName("add");

        // Create the parameters to pass to the add method.
        // Notice that we are creating Integer objects, which
        // are automatically bound to the xsd:int data type
        Object[] params = { new Integer(3), new Integer(4)};

        // Now, we call the add method, passing in the two
        // integers.
        System.out.print("The result of 3+4 is ");
        System.out.println((Integer)call.invoke(params));
    } catch (Exception e)
    {
        System.err.println(e.toString());
    }
    }
}
}
```

Unfortunately, as you can see in Example 3-2, the code contains a lot of bookkeeping (in particular, potentially dangerous casting). Also, there is no way for an IDE to assist with the development of dynamic client code; remote method names are passed as hardcoded strings. Most programming languages support accessing SOAP-based web services in this fashion.

Static SOAP Client

A *static* SOAP client uses a provided WSDL to generate a set of corresponding Java classes. This makes it easier to build and maintain an application, allowing for stricter type information and less bookkeeping. It also makes it easier for an IDE to assist you in your development (e.g., providing automatic code completion).

To generate client-side Java objects that can access the remote SOAP service we just created, run the Axis WSDL2Java tool as shown in Example 3-3.

Example 3-3. Axis client stub generation

```
C:\devenv\axis-1_1\lib>java -classpath commons-logging.jar;
    log4j-1.2.8.jar;wsdl4j.jar;axis.jar;commons-discovery.jar;
    jaxrpc.jar;saaj.jar
  org.apache.axis.wsdl.WSDL2Java -p localhost
    http://localhost:8080/axis/CurrentDate.jws?wsdl
```

The command shown in Example 3-3 should be entered as a single line, and if successful there will be no visible output (make sure Tomcat is running before running this command). Four files are generated as shown in Figure 3-10.

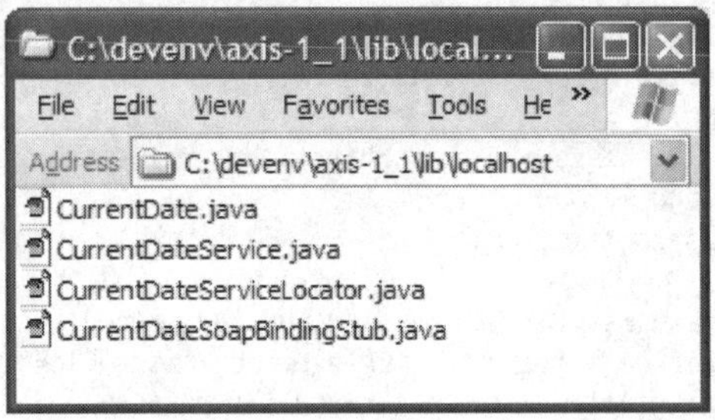

Figure 3-10. Generated client stub files

You'll want to copy the *localhost* directory to your source directory. Make sure you don't manually make changes to these source files; they are machine-generated, and they should be regenerated using WSDL2Java if changes to the WSDL are made (you may wish to automate this process using an Ant task: see *http://ws.apache.org/axis/java/ant/axis-wsdl2java.html*).

Example 3-4 shows a simple static client that uses the bindings generated by WSDL2Java. Notice the lack of casting and the natural passing of parameters to the add( ) method. The flow of the code is straightforward and common to other Axis-generated bindings used in this book; a Locator object is used to retrieve a Service. Methods called on the returned Service actually make requests to the remote service. Consider the underlying work being performed by the myDate.add(3, 4) line in the example shown: the parameters are bundled, transformed into a SOAP message, and sent; and the result is retrieved, converted back into a Java object, and returned.

Example 3-4. Static Axis client

```
package com.cascadetg.ch03;
import localhost.*;

public class StaticCurrentDateClient
{
```

Example 3-4. Static Axis client (continued)

```
    public static void main(String[] args)
    {
        CurrentDateService myService =
            new CurrentDateServiceLocator( );
        try
        {
            CurrentDate myDate = myService.getCurrentDate( );

            System.out.print(
                "According to the web service, it is now ");

            System.out.println(myDate.now( ));

            System.out.print("The result of 3+4 is ");
            System.out.println(myDate.add(3, 4));

        } catch (Exception e)
        {
            e.printStackTrace( );
        }

    }
}
```

In the remainder of this book, we access SOAP-based web services using the static method because it provides for a safer, easier method of access.

When WSDL Changes

You may be wondering how applications using statically generated bindings are affected when changes occur to the WSDL. Generally speaking, they work as you would expect; removing methods causes problems for applications that uses the methods, changes to signatures cause the problems you would expect, and new methods aren't called if not needed.

Applications can respond to WSDL changes much more effectively if they use generated bindings. Consider a WSDL file that adds a method: if the new method is needed, a new set of binding can instantly be generated. If a WSDL removes a method or changes a signature when the bindings are regenerated, the now-broken usage of that method appears as a compilation error. If dynamic bindings are used, there is no way to know that a failure was waiting until runtime, and finding out there is a problem on a production server is far worse than a compile-time error.

Other Platforms

You shouldn't labor under any illusion that web services can be accessed only via Java (or the Apache libraries described in this chapter). The combination of Java and

Apache merely provides for a free, reasonably robust, popular development platform. There are a variety of options, and depending on your situation, one of these may be more appropriate.

Note that virtually every programming language offers support for XML-RPC; please see *http://www.xmlrpc.com/directory/1568/implementations* for a list of implementations, including AppleScript, C, C++, Cold Fusion, COM, Dylan, Eiffel, Flash, JavaScript, Lingo, Lisp, Perl, PHP, Python, REALBasic, Rebol, Tcl, and many more.

PHP

PHP (*http://www.php.net*) is a popular language for web application development; it's easy, it's fun, and it integrates very well with databases such as MySQL. PHP offers excellent services for dealing with the network and HTTP. PEAR::SOAP at *http://pear.php.net/package/SOAP* is a popular, reasonably well-maintained SOAP implementation for PHP.

Perl

Perl support for SOAP as both a client and a server can be found at *http://www. soaplite.com/*. For more information on Perl and web services, see *Programming Web Services with Perl* (O'Reilly).

Microsoft

Microsoft has made web services a significant part of it's overall strategy, encompassing a variety of products and technologies. It's well beyond the scope of this text to delve into the full range of Microsoft's support for web services; for more information, visit *http://msdn.microsoft.com/webservices/*.

Note that Microsoft's aggressive support for SOAP can be hard for other vendors to match; if you are building a server using Microsoft SOAP technologies, make sure you enable services that other SOAP implementations can access.

Project 1: Competitive Analysis

If you sell products, you're almost certainly interested in watching the market for similar products. Consider one example of this: someone who monitors the book market, keeping track of the performance of a set of titles over time. This chapter shows how to use web services to pull together reports on product information from three different sources—Amazon, Google, and eBay. You'll build a simple web application that will let an analyst enter product information and have a report emailed that contains the relevant information.

Application Features

Here's the basic feature set:

- User enters and saves search information for a book (the title and an ISBN).
- User can create, view, delete, and run saved searches.

The application tracks the following data:

- Amazon.com prices, availability, release date, and sales rank based on the supplied ISBN
- Google rankings and top five search results for the book title
- eBay search results for the book title, including number of matching listings, highest price, and number of bids

A few JSP pages can present the information and accept input from the user. These JSP pages rely on a simple Java class, Search. The Search class deals with connections to web services via a set of supporting classes: AmazonConnection, EbayConnection, and GoogleConnection. This relationship is shown in Figure 4-1.

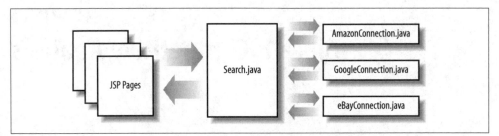

Figure 4-1. Interaction between JSPs and Java support and connection classes

First, the following list details the JSP pages and presentation objects used in the application.

list.jsp
> A list of the previously saved searches

new.jsp
> Create a new search

view.jsp
> View the results of a search

delete.jsp
> Delete a saved search

update.jsp
> Request an existing search to be updated

default.css
> Rudimentary stylesheet

Listing Searches

The first JSP, *list.jsp*, is shown in Figure 4-2. This is the main page for the web application. Clicking View takes users to a report page showing the data retrieved from the various web services. Delete removes the selected search from the web application, and Update causes the web application to refresh the data from the various web services.

The code for *list.jsp* is shown in Example 4-1. It can conceptually be broken into three main sections. First, there are a few initialization lines, the normal JSP and HTML headers. Next, a JSP scriptlet retrieves data from our supporting Java classes and performs some housekeeping to more cleanly present the data in the JSP. Finally, the actual HTML formatting and JSP display variables appear.

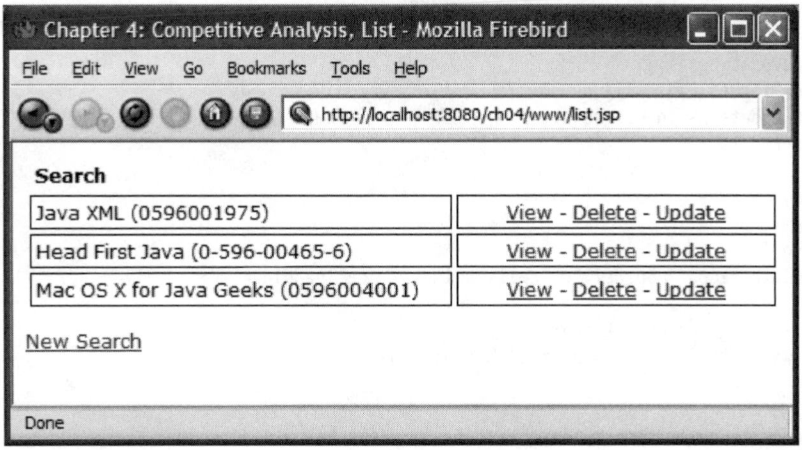

Figure 4-2. Listing searches

Example 4-1. Main search results JSP

```jsp
<%@ page contentType="text/html; charset=iso-8859-1" language="java"
 import="com.cascadetg.ch04.*" errorPage="" %>
<%

    boolean isUpdating = false;

    java.util.Hashtable mySearches
        = com.cascadetg.ch04.Search.getAllSearches( );
    if(mySearches != null)
    {
        java.util.Enumeration mySearchEnum = mySearches.elements( );

        while(mySearchEnum.hasMoreElements( ))
        {
            Search current =
                (com.cascadetg.ch04.Search)mySearchEnum.nextElement( );
            if(current.isUpdating( ))
                isUpdating = true;
        }
    }

%>
<html xmlns="http://www.w3.org/1999/xhtml">
<head>
<title>Chapter 4: Competitive Analysis, List</title>
<meta http-equiv="Content-Type"
    content="text/html; charset=iso-8859-1" />
<% if (isUpdating) { %>
<meta http-equiv="refresh" content="15;url=list.jsp">
<% } %>
<link href="default.css" rel="stylesheet" type="text/css" />
</head>
```

Example 4-1. Main search results JSP (continued)

```
<body>
<% if (isUpdating) { %>
<p align="right">Page will automatic refresh every 15 seconds
while an update is in progress.</p>
<% } %>

<% if (mySearches == null) { %>
<p>No searches defined.</p>
<% } else { %>
<table width="100%"  border="0" cellspacing="3" cellpadding="3">
  <tr>
    <td><strong>Search</strong></td>
    <td width="200" nowrap="nowrap"> </td>
  </tr>
<%
    java.util.Enumeration mySearchListing = mySearches.elements();
    while(mySearchListing.hasMoreElements())
    {
        Search mySearch = (Search)mySearchListing.nextElement();
        String productID = mySearch.getProductID();
        %>
  <tr>
    <td class="list">
        <%= mySearch.getProductTitle() %> (<%= productID %>)</td>
    <td width="200" align="center" nowrap="nowrap" class="list">
    <a href="view.jsp?productID=<%=productID %>">View</a> -
    <a href="delete.jsp?productID=<%=productID %>">Delete</a> -
    <a href="update.jsp?productID=<%=productID %>">Update</a></td>
  </tr>
<%
    }
%>
</table>
<% } %>
<p><a href="new.jsp">New Search</a></p>
</body>
</html>
```

Adding Searches

A user can click on the New Search link (as shown in Figure 4-2) to be brought to a form to add a new search. An example of this form is shown in Figure 4-3.

The book title field is self-explanatory. The ISBN field is provided to allow entry of an International Standard Book Number (ISBN), a worldwide standard for providing a unique identifying number for any published book.

The ISBN number can typically be found on the back cover of a book. You can also find ISBN numbers for books by browsing the Amazon web site or consulting with

Browser window showing:

Chapter 4: Competitive Analysis - Mozilla Firebird

File   Edit   View   Go   Bookmarks   Tools   Help

http://localhost:8080/ch04/www/new.jsp

Book ISBN :

Book Title :

Submit

Add Mac OS X for Java Geeks

Done

Figure 4-3. Adding a new search

the publisher. If you just want to try the application without finding a new ISBN, you can click on the provided link.

Another, different standard from ISBN is the Universal Product Code (UPC). Often, both the creator and distributors of a product introduce additional identifying codes for goods and services. Which codes to use is usually a business-driven question, but you'll want to be aware of what numbering systems are in place.

In this example, we're using the ISBN as the unique identifier for the books we're searching for, but in the "real world," you may want to use your own internal tracking system and then map that to the other systems. For example, if you carry both books (ISBN) and pickles (UPC), you're using two different numbering systems.

The code for *new.jsp* file is fairly straightforward, as shown in Example 4-2. If the creation of a new search is successful, users are returned to *list.jsp*.

Example 4-2. New search JSP

```
<%@ page contentType="text/html; charset=iso-8859-1"
language="java" errorPage="" %>
<%
    boolean success = false;
    boolean submitted = (request.getParameter("Submit") != null);
    if(submitted)
    {
        String productID = request.getParameter("productID");
        String productTitle = request.getParameter("productTitle");

        success =
            com.cascadetg.ch04.Search.addSearch(productID, productTitle);
        if(success)
        {
            response.sendRedirect("list.jsp");
```

Example 4-2. New search JSP (continued)

```
            return;
        }
    }
%>
<head>
<title>Chapter 4: Competitive Analysis</title>
<meta http-equiv="Content-Type"
    content="text/html; charset=iso-8859-1" />
<link href="default.css" rel="stylesheet" type="text/css" />
</head>
<body>
<% if(submitted) { %>
<p>Error submitting. Try again.</p>
<% } %>
<form name="new_item" id="new_item" method="post" action="new.jsp">
  <table width="60%"  border="0" cellspacing="0" cellpadding="0">
    <tr>
      <td width="50%">Book ISBN :</td>
      <td><input name="productID" type="text" /></td>
    </tr>
    <tr>
      <td width="50%">Book Title :</td>
      <td><input name="productTitle" type="text" /></td>
    </tr>
    <tr>
      <td width="50%"> </td>
      <td><input type="submit" name="Submit" value="Submit" /></td>
    </tr>
  </table>
  <p><a href="new.
jsp?productID=0596004001&productTitle=Mac%20OS%20X%20for%20Java%20Geeks&Submit=Submit">
  Add Mac OS X for Java Geeks</a> </p>
</form>
</body>
</html>
```

Viewing a Search

Figure 4-4 shows an example of the results of a search. The user can click the "Return to list" link in the upper-right corner to return to the search list.

As you can see from Example 4-3, *view.jsp* retrieves the results from the Search object. The results are then formatted into a HTML table. The heavy lifting is performed by the Search.update( ) method, as described later in this chapter.

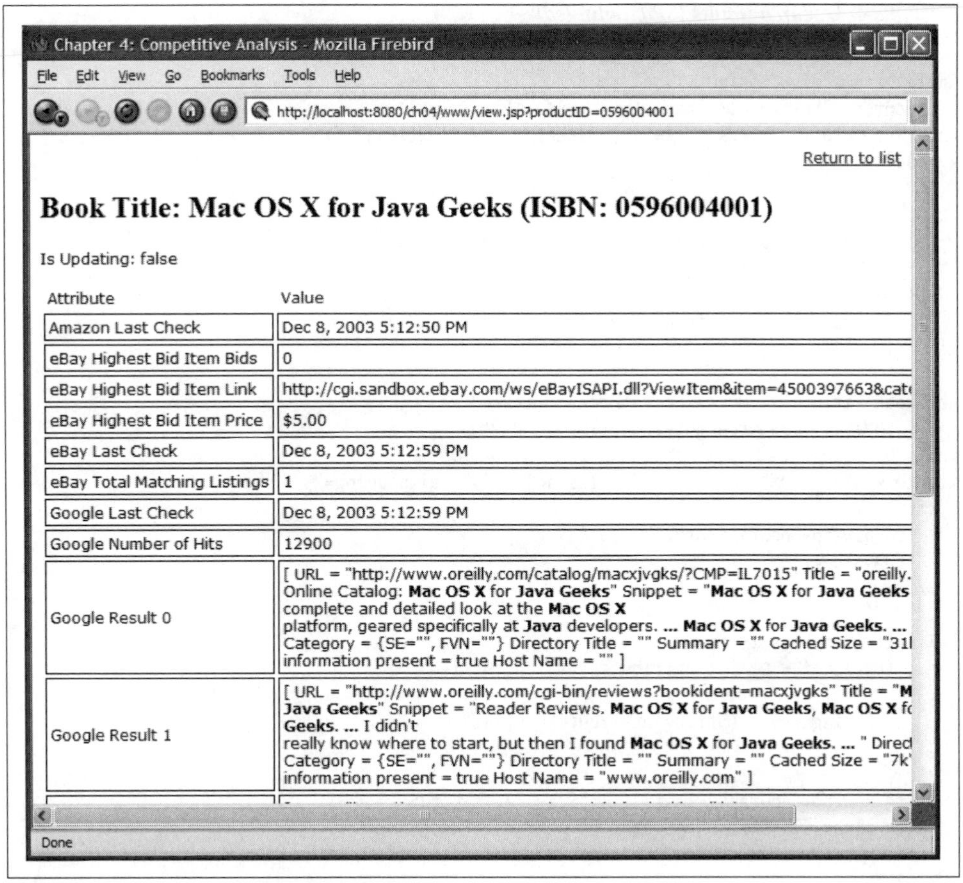

Return to list

Book Title: Mac OS X for Java Geeks (ISBN: 0596004001)

Is Updating: false

Attribute	Value
Amazon Last Check	Dec 8, 2003 5:12:50 PM
eBay Highest Bid Item Bids	0
eBay Highest Bid Item Link	http://cgi.sandbox.ebay.com/ws/eBayISAPI.dll?ViewItem&item=4500397663&cat(
eBay Highest Bid Item Price	$5.00
eBay Last Check	Dec 8, 2003 5:12:59 PM
eBay Total Matching Listings	1
Google Last Check	Dec 8, 2003 5:12:59 PM
Google Number of Hits	12900
Google Result 0	[URL = "http://www.oreilly.com/catalog/macxjvgks/?CMP=IL7015" Title = "oreilly. Online Catalog: **Mac OS X for Java Geeks**" Snippet = "**Mac OS X for Java Geeks** complete and detailed look at the **Mac OS X** platform, geared specifically at **Java** developers. ... Mac OS X for **Java Geeks**. ... Category = {SE="", FVN=""} Directory Title = "" Summary = "" Cached Size = "31 information present = true Host Name = ""]
Google Result 1	[URL = "http://www.oreilly.com/cgi-bin/reviews?bookident=macxjvgks" Title = "**M Java Geeks**" Snippet = "Reader Reviews. **Mac OS X for Java Geeks**, Mac OS X fo **Geeks**. ... I didn't really know where to start, but then I found **Mac OS X for Java Geeks**. ... " Direc Category = {SE="", FVN=""} Directory Title = "" Summary = "" Cached Size = "7k' information present = true Host Name = "www.oreilly.com"]

Done

Figure 4-4. Viewing search results

Example 4-3. Search results JSP

```
<%@ page contentType="text/html; charset=iso-8859-1"
language="java" errorPage="" %>
<%
    String productID = request.getParameter("productID");
    com.cascadetg.ch04.Search mySearch
        = com.cascadetg.ch04.Search.getSearch(productID);
    Object[] attributeKeys = null;
    if(mySearch != null)
    {
        java.util.Map myAttributes = mySearch.getAttributes();
        if(myAttributes != null)
        {
            attributeKeys = myAttributes.keySet().toArray();
        }
    };
%>
<head>
```

Example 4-3. Search results JSP (continued)

```
<title>Chapter 4: Competitive Analysis</title>
<meta http-equiv="Content-Type"
    content="text/html; charset=iso-8859-1" />
<link href="default.css" rel="stylesheet" type="text/css" />
</head>

<body>
<p align="right"><a href="list.jsp">Return to list</a></p>
<% if(mySearch == null)
    { %>
    <p>Unable to find this product ID (<%=productID%>)</p>
<%    } else { %>

<h2>Book Title: <%= mySearch.getProductTitle( ) %>
    (ISBN: <%= mySearch.getProductID( ) %>)</h2>
<p>Is Updating: <%= mySearch.isUpdating( ) %></p>
<table width="100%"  border="0" cellspacing="3" cellpadding="3">
  <tr>
    <td nowrap="nowrap">Attribute</td>
    <td>Value</td>
  </tr>
  <%
  if(attributeKeys != null)
      for(int i = 0; i < attributeKeys.length; i++)
    {
        String key = (String)attributeKeys[i];
  %>
  <tr>
    <td nowrap="nowrap" class="list"><%= key %></td>
    <td class="list"><%= mySearch.getAttribute(key) %></td>
  </tr>
  <% } %>
</table>
<% } %>
<p><a href="list.jsp">Return to list</a></p>
<p><a href="new.jsp">New search</a></p>
</body>
</html>
```

Removing a Search

If we allow people to add searches, we also should allow them to remove them. When a user clicks delete from the main JSP (as shown in Figure 4-2), a simple form (as shown in Figure 4-5) prompts the user to confirm the deletion before processing the request.

The code for this delete confirmation dialog is shown in Example 4-4.

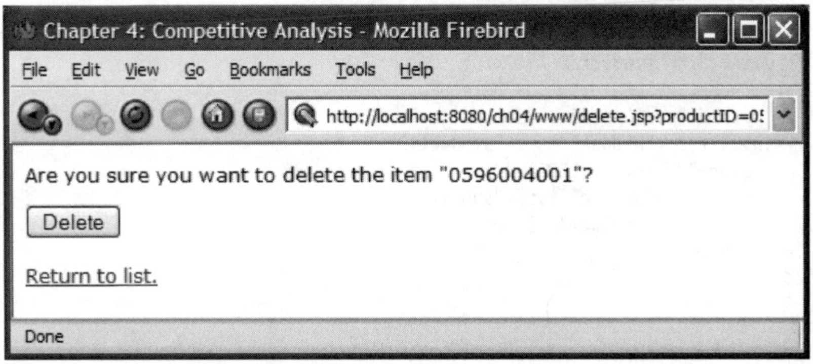

Figure 4-5. Delete confirmation web page

Example 4-4. Delete confirmation JSP code

```jsp
<%@ page contentType="text/html; charset=iso-8859-1"
language="java" errorPage="" %>
<%
    boolean delete = false;
    String productID = request.getParameter("productID");
    if(request.getParameter("Delete") != null)
        delete = true;

    boolean deleted = false;
    if(delete)
    {
        deleted =
            com.cascadetg.ch04.Search.removeSearch(productID);
    };
%>
<head>
<title>Chapter 4: Competitive Analysis</title>
<meta http-equiv="Content-Type"
    content="text/html; charset=iso-8859-1" />
<link href="default.css"
    rel="stylesheet" type="text/css" />
</head>
<body><%
if (delete)
{
    if(deleted)
    {
%>
        <p>The item has been deleted.</p>
<%    } else {
%>
        <p>Item not found.</p>
<%    }
} else{ %>
```

Example 4-4. Delete confirmation JSP code (continued)

```
            <p>Are you sure you want to delete the
                item "<%= productID %>"?</p>
            <form name="deleteForm" id="deleteForm"
                method="post" action="delete.jsp">
              <input type="hidden" name="productID"
                value="<%= productID %>"/>
              <input name="Delete" type="submit"
                id="Delete" value="Delete" />
            </form>
            <%
    }
%>
<p><a href="list.jsp">Return to list.</a></p>
</body>
</html>
```

Updating a Search

The Search object caches the data returned from the various web services in memory, but a user may wish to force the system to immediately refresh the data. Clicking on the update link on the main page (Figure 4-2) allows a user to do just that,
after a confirmation web page, as shown in Figure 4-6.

Figure 4-6. Confirming an update request

The code for the update confirmation page is shown in Example 4-5.

Example 4-5. Update confirmation JSP

```
<%@ page contentType="text/html; charset=iso-8859-1"
language="java" import="com.cascadetg.ch04.*" errorPage="" %>
<!DOCTYPE html PUBLIC "-//W3C//DTD XHTML 1.0 Transitional//EN"
"http://www.w3.org/TR/xhtml1/DTD/xhtml1-transitional.dtd">
<html xmlns="http://www.w3.org/1999/xhtml">
<head>
<%
    boolean updateProduct = false;
    String productID = request.getParameter("productID");
    if(productID != null)
```

Example 4-5. Update confirmation JSP (continued)

```
    {
        updateProduct = true;
        Search.getSearch(productID).update( );
    }

%>
<title>Chapter 4: Competitive Analysis</title>
<meta http-equiv="Content-Type"
content="text/html; charset=iso-8859-1" />
<link href="default.css" rel="stylesheet" type="text/css" />
</head>

<body>
<% if (updateProduct) { %>
<p>Product updated.</p>
<% } else { %>

<p>Unknown product.</p>
<% } %>
<p><a href="list.jsp">Return to list.</a> </p>
</body>
</html>
```

Gathering Web Service Data

The various user interface elements, as shown so far, all rely on a single Search class for the actual web service data retrieval; the JSP pages don't contain any code that actually communicates with web services. Instead, a single Search object relies on supporting classes, as shown in Figure 4-7, to retrieve the data.

The four static methods, addSearch( ), getAllSearches( ), getSearch( ), and removeSearch( ), are the main points of interest to the JSP pages. All data about the web services results is contained in a set of simple name/value pairs, contained in the java.util.Hashtable variable attributes. When a search is run, the Search object is passed to the three supporting web service connection classes, and the appropriate data is set in attributes.

The code shown in Example 4-6 shows the code for the Search class. Pay particular interest to the update( ) method.

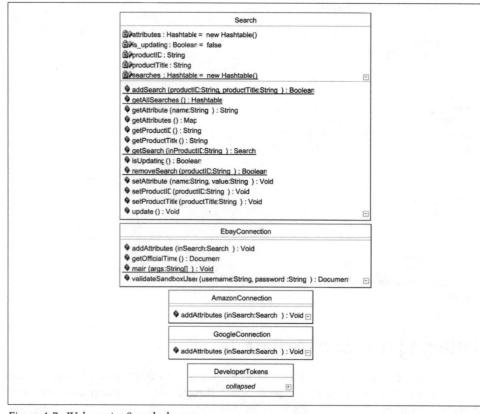

Figure 4-7. Web service Search classes

Example 4-6. Core Search class

```
package com.cascadetg.ch04;

import java.util.Hashtable;

public class Search
{
    // Static search Hashtable used for persistence.
    // This means that the data stored by this application is lost
    // every time the server is restarted. Adding support for
    // persistence is left as an exercise for the reader - the most
    // likely, of course, being saving the data to a database in some
    // fashion.

    // If you are interested in adding persistence, you'll want to
    // intercept the addSearch(), removeSearch(), and update() methods
    // in this class.

    private static Hashtable searches = new Hashtable();
```

Example 4-6. Core Search class (continued)

```java
    public static boolean addSearch(
        String productID,
        String productTitle)
    {
        if (productID == null)
            return false;
        if (productID.length() < 1)
            return false;
        if (productTitle == null)
            return false;
        if (productID.length() < 1)
            return false;

        if (searches.get(productID) != null)
            searches.remove(productID);

        Search mySearch = new Search();
        mySearch.setProductID(productID);
        mySearch.setProductTitle(productTitle);
        searches.put(productID, mySearch);
        mySearch.update();
        return true;
    }

    public static boolean removeSearch(String productID)
    {
        if (searches == null)
        {
            return true;
        }
        if (searches.get(productID) == null)
            return false;
        searches.remove(productID);
        return true;
    }

    public static Hashtable getAllSearches()
    {
        return searches;
    }

    public static Search getSearch(String inProductID)
    {
        return (Search)searches.get(inProductID);
    }

    // Simple object data. Note the use of a Hashtable to store
    // a variable set of attributes

    private String productID;
    private String productTitle;
    private Hashtable attributes = new Hashtable();
```

Example 4-6. Core Search class (continued)

```java
public void setAttribute(String name, String value)
{
    attributes.put(name, value);
}

public String getAttribute(String name)
{
    return (String)attributes.get(name);
}

public java.util.Map getAttributes( )
{

    java.util.TreeMap map =
        new java.util.TreeMap(java.text.Collator.getInstance( ));
    map.putAll(attributes);

    return map;
}

/** Returns the product ID (specifically, a book ISBN). */
public String getProductID( )
{
    return productID;
}

/** Set the product ID (specificially, a book ISBN). */
public void setProductID(String productID)
{
    this.productID = productID;
}

public String getProductTitle( )
{
    return productTitle;
}

public void setProductTitle(String productTitle)
{
    this.productTitle = productTitle;
}

// Updating data logic

// Note that this updating logic isn't as useful as it should be,
// as the update( ) ought to kick off a new thread.
private boolean is_updating = false;
public boolean isUpdating( )
{
    return is_updating;
}
```

Example 4-6. Core Search class (continued)

```
public void update( )
{
    // Don't allow the user to set up dozens of hits on the site at
    // once. Ideally, you should be more conservative about kicking
    // off requests, perhaps using an aggregation approach (as
    // described in Chapter 8, News Aggregator
    if (is_updating)
        return;
    is_updating = true;

    // Create a new Search and set the values to the existing
    // search
    Search mySearch = new Search( );
    mySearch.setProductID(this.productID);
    mySearch.setProductTitle(this.productTitle);

    // Kick off the requests to the various web services
    new AmazonConnection( ).addAttributes(mySearch);
    new EbayConnection( ).addAttributes(mySearch);
    new GoogleConnection( ).addAttributes(mySearch);

    // Replace the old attributes with the newly discovered values
    this.attributes = mySearch.attributes;

    is_updating = false;
    }
}
```

It's easy to imagine enhancements: the underlying system might implement a Connection interface, with the potential to add new web services dynamically.

One other thing you may have noticed: the getAttributes( ) method returns a java. util.Map, instead of the underlying Hashtable. As shown in Example 4-7, the code creates a TreeMap that keeps the attributes sorted by the system's default locale interpretation of an "alphabetical" sorting routine.

Example 4-7. Sorting code

```
java.util.TreeMap map =
new java.util.TreeMap(java.text.Collator.getInstance( ));
    map.putAll(attributes);
```

Now, on to the real meat of the application—the web services connectivity.

Connecting to Amazon

The Amazon web services package is implemented according to the commonly regarded interpretation of web services—a series of SOAP methods, complete with a WSDL file describing their offerings. We will use Axis, as described in Chapter 3, to work with Amazon's web services.

Before working with Amazon's web services, you must register with Amazon's developer program at *http://www.amazon.com/webservices/*, as shown in Figure 4-8.

Figure 4-8. Signing up for Amazon web services

The instructions are straightforward: you must download the developer kit (a single file, *kit.zip*) and get a web services token. This token, a simple string, is used by Amazon to uniquely identify you when you are accessing web services. You should treat this token as you would any password.

As shown in Figure 4-9, you'll find a number of examples for a variety of programming languages as well as the documentation.

Open the file *kit/API Guide/index.html* in your web browser to see the documentation, as shown in Figure 4-10.

In our case, we'll use Axis to generate access code from the Amazon-supplied WSDL file. The Amazon WSDL file, as described in the *READMEFIRST.txt* file, can be found at *http://soap.amazon.com/schemas3/AmazonWebServices.wsdl*. This WSDL file is used by the Axis WSDL2Java tool to generate a set of Java bindings. The easiest way to do this is to open a command prompt and navigate to the Axis library installation directory. Then, execute the following command, all as one line, as shown in Example 4-8. Note that you need an Internet connection for this to work.

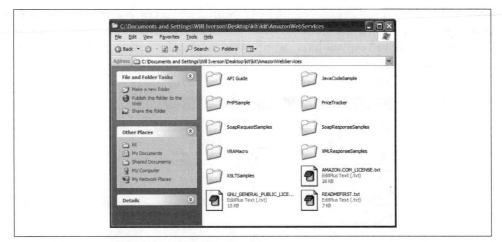

Figure 4-9. Contents of the Amazon SDK

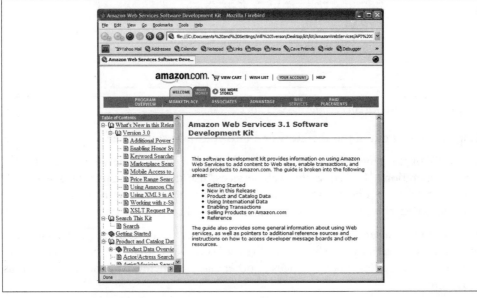

Figure 4-10. Amazon SDK documentation

Example 4-8. Generating Amazon Java bindings from WSDL

```
C:\devenv\axis-1_1\lib>java -classpath commons-logging.jar;
    log4j-1.2.8.jar;wsdl4j.jar;axis.jar;commons-discovery.jar;
    jaxrpc.jar;saaj.jar
  org.apache.axis.wsdl.WSDL2Java
    http://soap.amazon.com/schemas3/AmazonWebServices.wsdl
```

If successful, there will be no visible output on the command line, but you will now
have a set of Java classes corresponding to the Amazon SDK in the Axis directory. As

shown in Figure 4-11, these classes are neatly sorted into a com.amazon.soap package. Although you are given the source to these classes by this tool, you won't want to edit them manually. You will likely want to regenerate these files any time Amazon adds new functionality.

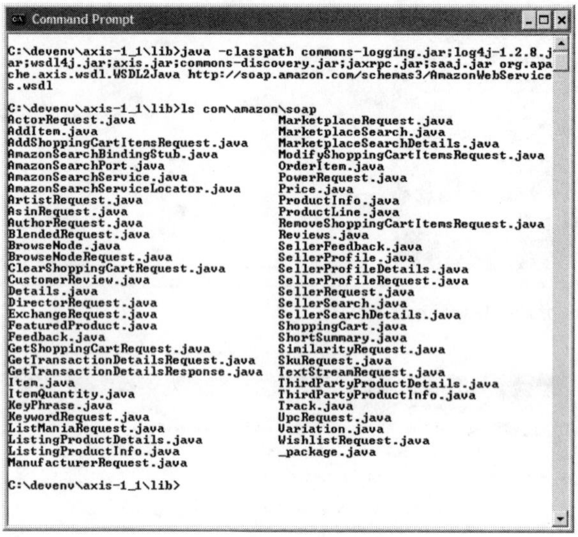

Figure 4-11. Generated Amazon Java Axis source

Copy these files out of this directory and into your Java source tree.

The bulk of the generated classes essentially serve as data holders for Amazon web service operations. To access the web services, use the AmazonSearchServiceLocator class to retrieve a service and an AmazonSearchPort to handle web service requests. The AmazonSearchServiceLocator class hierarchy is shown in Figure 4-12.

After retrieving a service, you use a search port object to perform requests. The generated class hierarchy is shown in Figure 4-13. Note that the methods of the AmazonSearchPort class take instances of other classes generated by the Axis toolkit as parameters.

The code shown in Example 4-9 shows how to actually make a connection to the Amazon web services. In this case, an instance of the AsinRequest class is used. The call to myAmazonSearchPort.asinSearchRequest(myAsinRequest) actually performs the request. It transforms the underlying data to SOAP, sends the data over the network, retrieves the resulting data, and transforms that data back into Java object(s), in this case a ProductInfo object.

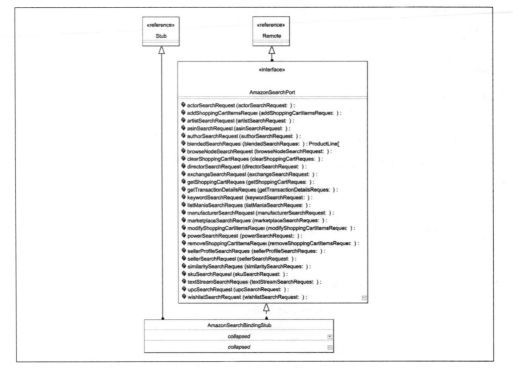

Figure 4-12. Amazon service locator class

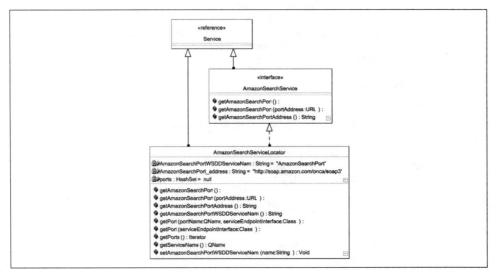

Figure 4-13. Amazon port request class

Example 4-9. Connecting to Amazon web services

```java
package com.cascadetg.ch04;

import java.util.Date;
import com.amazon.soap.*;

public class AmazonConnection
{

    public void addAttributes(Search inSearch)
    {
        inSearch.setAttribute(
            "Amazon Last Check",
            new Date().toLocaleString());

        // Mac OS X for Java Geeks ISBN
        //String isbn = "0596004001";

        try
        {
            AmazonSearchService myAmazonSearchService =
                new AmazonSearchServiceLocator();
            AmazonSearchPort myAmazonSearchPort =
                myAmazonSearchService.getAmazonSearchPort();

            AsinRequest myAsinRequest = new AsinRequest();

            // Use this to set your Amazon Associates ID
            // For more info on Amazon Associates, see...
            // http://www.amazon.com/associates
            myAsinRequest.setTag(DeveloperTokens.amazon_associates);
            myAsinRequest.setDevtag(DeveloperTokens.amazon_token);
            myAsinRequest.setAsin(inSearch.getProductID());
            myAsinRequest.setLocale("us");
            myAsinRequest.setType("heavy");

            ProductInfo myProductInfo =
                myAmazonSearchPort.asinSearchRequest(myAsinRequest);

            Details[] myDetailsArray = myProductInfo.getDetails();
            Details myDetail = null;
            if (myDetailsArray != null)
            {
                myDetail = myDetailsArray[0];

                inSearch.setAttribute(
                    "Amazon Product Name",
                    myDetail.getProductName());

                inSearch.setAttribute(
                    "Amazon Release Date",
                    myDetail.getReleaseDate());
```

Example 4-9. Connecting to Amazon web services (continued)

```
                    inSearch.setAttribute(
                        "Amazon Actual Prize",
                        myDetail.getOurPrice( ));

                    inSearch.setAttribute(
                        "Amazon List Price",
                        myDetail.getListPrice( ));

                    inSearch.setAttribute(
                        "Amazon Used Price",
                        myDetail.getUsedPrice( ));

                    inSearch.setAttribute(
                        "Amazon Sales Rank",
                        myDetail.getSalesRank( ));

                    inSearch.setAttribute(
                        "Amazon Availability",
                        myDetail.getAvailability( ));

                    //myDetail.getImageUrlSmall( );
                    //myDetail.getImageUrlMedium( );
                    //myDetail.getImageUrlLarge( );
                }
            } catch (Exception e)
            {
                e.printStackTrace( );

            }
        }
}
```

The code shown in Example 4-9 is as close to a standard RPC system as a web service is likely to be. None of the actual connectivity details are in the code: all of the URLs, ports, and other connectivity information are in the WSDL and then embedded in the code generated by the WSDL2Java tool.

Connecting to eBay

eBay's web service implementation provides access to their systems via XML over HTTPS. A simple HTTPS connection provides in-transit security, and XML data is sent and received to perform operations. While establishing an HTTPS connection to the eBay servers is a relatively trivial matter, working with the XML documents is more time-consuming.

As of mid-2004, there are several tiers of access offered by eBay, based more or less on the quantity of web service requests you require. The free, individual developer version allows for only 50 calls a day—not very many, but likely enough to build and do some basic testing of your application. The next step up, called Basic, offers 30,000 calls per month for $500 per year.

By default, you have access to the eBay *sandbox* server, a test environment set up for developers to test their application without incurring service fees. To access the production server, you must be certified by eBay (as of this writing, eBay charges $100 for certification). If you're looking at building a production application that accesses eBay services, you need to include these access and certification fees in your budget. Don't forget that it can take several days to get your application certified.

The eBay sandbox, *http://sandbox.ebay.com/*, shown in Figure 4-14, is a good development resource. It's a recreation of the eBay web site (*http://www.ebay.com/*) and is intended for developers to test their application. There are several portions of the web site that aren't implemented or work slightly differently; for example, you can't actually enter a credit card and authenticate a user to sell items on the test server. Instead, you use eBay web services to do this programmatically using the web services API.

The eBay developer registration system is a bit more complex than other offerings in order to support more complex deployment and usage models. First, you need to register for eBay itself and then go through the six-step registration process (*http://developer.ebay.com/* → *Membership* → *Join*). When you're done registering, you can generate a set of three security tokens, a Developer ID (devID), Application ID (appID), and Certification ID (certID). Make sure that your pop-up blocking software is disabled when you generate your security tokens.

 Don't lose your eBay security tokens! You can generate them for the first time online, but if you lose them, you'll have to go through eBay support. It can take several days to verify your information and receive new tokens.

Figure 4-14. eBay sandbox site

eBay API wrapper

In order to make it easier to connect to eBay in this chapter (and others), the sample applications use a standard eBay connectivity class, as shown in Figure 4-15, as a reusable component for connecting to eBay's XML-via-HTTPS web services.

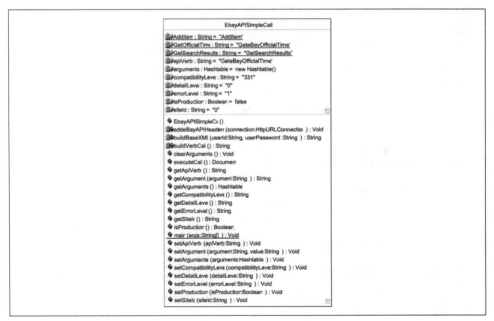

Figure 4-15. eBay web service utility class

The code for the eBay class is shown in Example 4-10. All the details of opening a connection to eBay, sending the XML, and then retrieving the results are wrapped by this class. The code is designed to make a call as simple as possible: create a new EbayAPISimpleCall object, set the eBay "verb" you wish to call, and add the arguments you need with EbayAPISimpleCall.setArgument( ).

Example 4-10. eBay API simple call

```java
package com.cascadetg.ch04;

import java.net.*;
import java.io.*;
import java.util.Hashtable;

/**
 * Based on the eBay sample code, APISimpleCallJava.java
 */

public class EbayAPISimpleCall
{

    // The eBay API function
    private String apiVerb = "GetebayOfficialTime";

    /** API Verb used to get the official eBay time */
    public static final String GetOfficialTime = "GetebayOfficialTime";
    /** API Verb used to search on eBay */
    public static final String GetSearchResults = "GetSearchResults";

    // The version threshold of compatibility for the eBay API call
    private String compatibilityLevel = "331";

    // The error level for the API call
    private String errorLevel = "1";

    // Set siteId to correspond to the US Site
    private String siteId = "0";

    // "0" is the only supported detail level for GetebayOfficialTime
    private String detailLevel = "0";

    public EbayAPISimpleCall()
    {
    }

    boolean isProduction = false;

    public org.jdom.Document executeCall()
    {
        // Supply a URL to the desired API server, for example:
        // Sandbox: https://api.sandbox.ebay.com/ws/api.dll
        // Production: https://api.ebay.com/ws/api.dll
        String targetURL;
```

Example 4-10. eBay API simple call (continued)

```
if (!isProduction)
{
    targetURL = "https://api.sandbox.ebay.com/ws/api.dll";
} else
{
    targetURL = "https://api.ebay.com/ws/api.dll";
}

// This string will contain the assembled XML for the API call
String eBayXML;

try
{

    // Create a new URL object using the specified targetURL
    URL website = new URL(targetURL);

    // Create a connection to the URL
    Object foo = website.openConnection();

    // Note that this is actually an SSL connection, even
    // though cast to an HttpURLConnection. Different JDK
    // versions use a different SSL connection class, but they
    // all use HttpURLConnection as the base class (which has
    // the methods we need).
    HttpURLConnection connection =
        (HttpURLConnection)website.openConnection();

    // Specify that the connection will be used for input and
    // output
    connection.setDoInput(true);
    connection.setDoOutput(true);

    // Specify the method for the URL request
    connection.setRequestMethod("POST");

    // Add the eBay specific headers needed for an eBay API
    // call
    // see: "Making the HTTP request" in the eBay API
    // documentation
    addeBayAPIHeaders(connection);

    // Build the XML call String for eBayGetOfficialTime
    eBayXML =
        buildBaseXML(
            DeveloperTokens.eBay_userid,
            DeveloperTokens.ebay_userPassword)
            + buildVerbCall();

    // Create the Output and Print Streams
    OutputStream output = connection.getOutputStream();
    PrintStream pout = new PrintStream(output);
```

Example 4-10. eBay API simple call (continued)

```
                // 'Upload' the eBayXML String
                pout.print(eBayXML);
                pout.close( );

                // Create the Input Streams
                InputStream input = connection.getInputStream( );
                BufferedInputStream bufIn = new BufferedInputStream(input);

                org.jdom.Document result =
                    new org.jdom.input.SAXBuilder( ).build(bufIn);
                connection.disconnect( );
                return result;

        } catch (MalformedURLException ex)
        {
            ex.printStackTrace( );
        } catch (IOException ioException)
        {
            ioException.printStackTrace( );
        } catch (org.jdom.JDOMException JDOMprob)
        {
            JDOMprob.printStackTrace( );
        }

        return null;
    }

    // A test routine to verify that everything is working.
    public static void main(String[] args) throws IOException
    {
        EbayAPISimpleCall myCall = new EbayAPISimpleCall( );
        myCall.setApiVerb(GetOfficialTime);
        org.jdom.Document myDocument = myCall.executeCall( );
        new org.jdom.output.XMLOutputter( ).output(
            myDocument,
            System.out);
        myCall.setApiVerb(GetSearchResults);
        myCall.setArgument("Query", "test");
        myDocument = myCall.executeCall( );
        new org.jdom.output.XMLOutputter( ).output(
            myDocument,
            System.out);

        String result =
            myDocument.getRootElement( ).getChild("eBayTime").getText( );
        System.out.println(result);

        result =
            myDocument
                .getRootElement( )
                .getChild("Search")
```

Example 4-10. eBay API simple call (continued)

```java
            .getChild("GrandTotal")
            .getText( );
    System.out.println(result);
}

private void addeBayAPIHeaders(HttpURLConnection connection)
{
    // Generate and add the Session Certificate Header
    connection.addRequestProperty(
        "X-EBAY-API-SESSION-CERTIFICATE",
        DeveloperTokens.ebay_devId
            + ";"
            + DeveloperTokens.appId
            + ";"
            + DeveloperTokens.certId);

    // Add the Compatibility Level Header
    connection.addRequestProperty(
        "X-EBAY-API-COMPATIBILITY-LEVEL",
        compatibilityLevel);

    // Add the Developer Name, Application Name, and Certification
    // Name headers
    connection.addRequestProperty(
        "X-EBAY-API-DEV-NAME",
        DeveloperTokens.ebay_devId);
    connection.addRequestProperty(
        "X-EBAY-API-APP-NAME",
        DeveloperTokens.appId);
    connection.addRequestProperty(
        "X-EBAY-API-CERT-NAME",
        DeveloperTokens.certId);

    // Add the API verb Header
    connection.addRequestProperty("X-EBAY-API-CALL-NAME", apiVerb);

    // Add the Site Id Header
    connection.addRequestProperty("X-EBAY-API-SITEID", siteId);

    // Add the Detail Level Header
    connection.addRequestProperty(
        "X-EBAY-API-DETAIL-LEVEL",
        detailLevel);

    // Add the Content-Type Header
    connection.addRequestProperty("Content-Type", "text/xml");

    // NOTE: eBay recommends setting the Content-Length header
    // see: "Making the HTTP request" in the eBay API documentation
}
```

Example 4-10. eBay API simple call (continued)

```
private String buildBaseXML(String userId, String userPassword)
{
    return "<?xml version='1.0' encoding='utf-8'?>\r\n"
        + "<request>\r\n"
        + "<RequestUserId>"
        + userId
        + "</RequestUserId>\r\n"
        + "<RequestPassword>"
        + userPassword
        + "</RequestPassword>\r\n";
}

Hashtable arguments = new Hashtable();
public void clearArguments()
{
    arguments = new Hashtable();
}

public Hashtable getArguments()
{
    return arguments;
}
public void setArgument(String argument, String value)
{
    arguments.put(argument, value);
}
public String getArgument(String argument)
{
    return (String)arguments.get(argument);
}
public void setArguments(Hashtable arguments)
{
    this.arguments = arguments;
}

private String buildVerbCall()
{
    StringBuffer verbCall = new StringBuffer();
    verbCall.append("<ErrorLevel>");
    verbCall.append(errorLevel);
    verbCall.append("</ErrorLevel>\r\n");
    verbCall.append("<Verb>");
    verbCall.append(apiVerb);
    verbCall.append("</Verb>\r\n");
    verbCall.append("<DetailLevel>");
    verbCall.append(detailLevel);
    verbCall.append("</DetailLevel>\r\n");
    verbCall.append("<SiteId>");
    verbCall.append(siteId);
    verbCall.append("</SiteId>\r\n");
    if (arguments.size() > 0)
    {
```

Example 4-10. eBay API simple call (continued)

```java
            java.util.Enumeration keys = arguments.keys();
            while (keys.hasMoreElements())
            {
                String current = (String)keys.nextElement();
                verbCall.append("<");
                verbCall.append(current);
                verbCall.append(">");
                verbCall.append(arguments.get(current));
                verbCall.append("</");
                verbCall.append(current);
                verbCall.append(">");
            }

        }

        verbCall.append("</request>");

        return verbCall.toString();
    }

    /**
     * @return Returns the detailLevel.
     */
    public String getDetailLevel()
    {
        return detailLevel;
    }

    /**
     * @param detailLevel
     *              The detailLevel to set.
     */
    public void setDetailLevel(String detailLevel)
    {
        this.detailLevel = detailLevel;
    }

    /**
     * @return Returns the errorLevel.
     */
    public String getErrorLevel()
    {
        return errorLevel;
    }

    /**
     * @param errorLevel
     *              The errorLevel to set.
     */
    public void setErrorLevel(String errorLevel)
    {
```

Example 4-10. eBay API simple call (continued)

```java
        this.errorLevel = errorLevel;
    }

    /**
     * @return Returns the siteId.
     */
    public String getSiteId( )
    {
        return siteId;
    }

    /**
     * @param siteId
     *             The siteId to set.
     */
    public void setSiteId(String siteId)
    {
        this.siteId = siteId;
    }

    /**
     * @return Returns the compatibilityLevel.
     */
    public String getCompatibilityLevel( )
    {
        return compatibilityLevel;
    }

    /**
     * @param compatibilityLevel
     *             The compatibilityLevel to set. This controls the
     *             versioning of the XML interface for the API. This is
     *             how eBay allows multiple versions of their API to be
     *             supported simultaneously.
     */
    public void setCompatibilityLevel(String compatibilityLevel)
    {
        this.compatibilityLevel = compatibilityLevel;
    }

    /**
     * @return Returns the isProduction.
     */
    public boolean isProduction( )
    {
        return isProduction;
    }

    /**
     * @param isProduction
     *             By default (isProduction = false), the server will
     *             contact the eBay test environment, called the
```

Example 4-10. eBay API simple call (continued)

```
*             "sandbox." If you wish to use the production
*             environment, you'll need to set this to true.
*/
public void setProduction(boolean isProduction)
{
    this.isProduction = isProduction;
}

public String getApiVerb( )
{
    return apiVerb;
}

/**
 * Two standard verbs are provided with this class,
 * GeteBayOfficialTime and GetSearchResults. Others can be added
 * from the eBay documentation.
 */
public void setApiVerb(String apiVerb)
{
    this.apiVerb = apiVerb;
}
}
```

For eBay, a *verb* is the term that describes the name of a web service method. Each verb describes a particular action, with a set of one or more possible parameters. These verbs generally have self-describing names, such as GeteBayOfficialTime or GetSearchResults. eBay's documentation lists many verbs; using our EbayAPISimpleCall. setApiVerb( ) method, it's easy to call any of them. Two static String objects are defined in this class; they correspond to the official eBay verbs. An enterprising developer might imagine developing a custom class hierarchy corresponding to the eBay framework. However, keep in mind that this class hierarchy quickly looks like the bindings generated by a SOAP framework!

When you're ready, call EbayAPISimpleCall.executeCall( ), and you'll receive a result via a JDOM object (which holds the XML returned by eBay). If the result is an eBay error message, that is the contents of the XML; otherwise, it should be the data you need.

The code to make the call into eBay is only support infrastructure; it doesn't actually help you write your application. It's analogous to the code generated by the WSDL2Java code in the previous example (talking to Amazon), but in this case, you have to maintain it yourself.

eBay connectivity

Now that you have a reusable wrapper for accessing eBay web services, it's time to look at the code to actually get useful data back from the eBay service.

As mentioned earlier, you must create and validate a user on the sandbox in order to perform certain activities, such as searches. The main( ) method of the code shown in Example 4-11 can be used to authenticate a user as a command-line utility if needed. The addAttributes( ) method is called by the Search object to retrieve data from eBay—a straightforward operation, given the wrapper shown in Example 4-10.

Example 4-11. Retrieving data from eBay

```
package com.cascadetg.ch04;

import java.util.Date;
import org.jdom.output.XMLOutputter;

public class EbayConnection
{

    public org.jdom.Document validateSandboxUser(
        String username,
        String password)
    {
        EbayAPISimpleCall myCall = new EbayAPISimpleCall( );
        // Validate this user on the sandbox server only
        myCall.setProduction(false);
        myCall.setApiVerb("ValidateTestUserRegistration");
        myCall.setArgument("RequestUserId", username);
        myCall.setArgument("RequestPassword", password);
        return myCall.executeCall( );
    }

    /**
     * Call this class, passing in the username and password you would
     * like to register on the eBay test server.
     *
     * @param args
     */
    static public void main(String[] args)
    {
        if (args == null)
        {
```

Example 4-11. Retrieving data from eBay (continued)

```
            System.out.println("Need two arguments (name & password).");
            return;
        }
        if (args.length < 2)
        {
            System.out.println("Need two arguments (name & password).");
            return;
        }
        try
        {
            new XMLOutputter( ).output(
                new EbayConnection( ).validateSandboxUser(
                    args[0],
                    args[1]),
                System.out);
        } catch (Exception e)
        {
            System.out.println("Unable to register user.");
            e.printStackTrace( );
        }
    }

    public void addAttributes(Search inSearch)
    {
        inSearch.setAttribute(
            "eBay Last Check",
            new Date( ).toLocaleString( ));

        EbayAPISimpleCall myCall = new EbayAPISimpleCall( );
        myCall.setApiVerb(EbayAPISimpleCall.GetSearchResults);
        myCall.setArgument("Query", inSearch.getProductTitle( ));
        myCall.setArgument("Order", "MetaHighestPriceSort");
        org.jdom.Document myResults = myCall.executeCall( );

        org.jdom.Element root = myResults.getRootElement( );
        long count =
            Long.parseLong(
                root
                    .getChild("Search")
                    .getChild("GrandTotal")
                    .getText( ));
        inSearch.setAttribute(
            "eBay Total Matching Listings",
            Long.toString(count));

        if (count > 0)
        {
            org.jdom.Element item =
                root.getChild("Search").getChild("Items").getChild(
                    "Item");
```

Example 4-11. Retrieving data from eBay (continued)

```
        inSearch.setAttribute(
            "eBay Highest Bid Item Price",
            item.getChildText("LocalizedCurrentPrice"));

        inSearch.setAttribute(
            "eBay Highest Bid Item Bids",
            item.getChildText("BidCount"));

        inSearch.setAttribute(
            "eBay Highest Bid Item Link",
            item.getChildText("Link"));
    }
  }
}
```

Authorizing a Sandbox User Account

Let's say that you want to test the system's search capability by adding a new item (for example, you'd like to add my book, *Mac OS X for Java Geeks*, so it will show up in a search). Or, you'd like to create a seller and a couple of buyers on the sandbox to test the full flow of an auction.

To do either activity, you must mark a user account on the sandbox server as an authorized seller. Start by using the web interface on *http://sandbox.ebay.com/* to create a user. Note that you can't go through the seller authentication mechanism via your web browser: it will fail at the end with a warning.

Instead, after you've created a user account, use the code in *EbayConnection.java* to authorize the account as a seller. Assuming everything is compiled and working properly, just execute this command:

```
java -classpath .;..\lib\jdom.jar com.cascadetg.ch04.EbayConnection username
password
```

This registers the user as having been validated on the eBay server.

Lets take a closer look at the connectivity code, as shown in Example 4-12. It starts by creating a object to represent the call to eBay, EbayAPISimpleCall. It then sets the eBay verb to use. In the sample, a search is being performed, but you can find documentation on other supported verbs at *http://developer.ebay.com/DevZone/docs/API_Doc/index.asp*.

Next, the arguments are set. For a search query, the search terms must be specified—in this case, the title of the book. The application also needs the highest value auction result, so a second argument, Order, is added with the string MetaHighestPriceSort (as specified by the eBay documentation for the search verb). The call is then issued, and an XML document containing the results of the query is returned. From there, it's just a question of using the JDOM interfaces to walk through the returned XML.

Example 4-12. eBay connection code.

```
EbayAPISimpleCall myCall = new EbayAPISimpleCall( );
myCall.setApiVerb(EbayAPISimpleCall.GetSearchResults);
myCall.setArgument("Query", inSearch.getProductTitle( ));
myCall.setArgument("Order", "MetaHighestPriceSort");
org.jdom.Document myResults = myCall.executeCall( );
```

To more fully support this, you may wish to perform more robust error handling (indeed, you'll be required to do this to pass eBay's certification), but it shows how even with a nonstandard API, a bit of work can decouple the details of establishing the network connection from the rest of your application logic.

Connecting to Google

After the previous examples, it may surprise you to see how easy it is to connect to Google's web service offerings. Visiting *http://www.google.com/apis/*, shown in Figure 4-16, it's pretty straightforward to start building applications using the Google web service interface. Make sure you download the developer kit as shown on the front page; you will need the provided libraries.

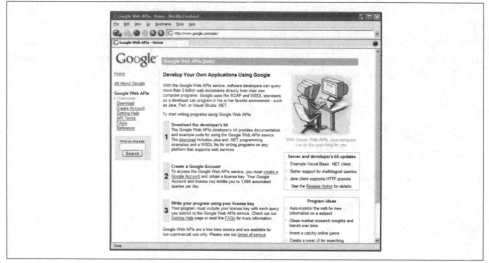

Figure 4-16. Google API home page

Google does offer APIs via SOAP and WSDL, but for Java developers, there's a pre-built library that does all the work for you. It's as if they took the time to run Axis WSDL2Java for you, and then just provided you with a library to use (in fact, that's very close to what they actually did). It's entirely possible to use Axis to generate the

Java code from their WSDL file (posted at *http://api.google.com/GoogleSearch.wsdl*) just as you did for Amazon. Instead, you should rely on the Java library they provided, called *googleapi.jar*, as shown in Figure 4-17. You must add this library to your class path. For more information on the Google API, open the *APIs_Reference. html* file.

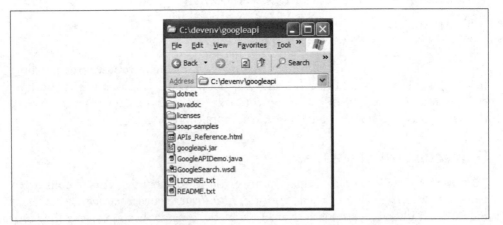

Figure 4-17. Contents of the Google SDK

The code as shown in Example 4-13 could hardly be simpler. More lines are spent looping through the results and adding them to the Search object's attributes than it takes to get data back from the Google server itself. The code converts the GoogleSearchResult objects to Strings and add them to the results given, but it's easy to imagine using the various methods on the GoogleSearchResult object to get more detail and provide even better formatting.

Example 4-13. Google connectivity

```
package com.cascadetg.ch04;
import java.util.Date;
import com.google.soap.search.*;

public class GoogleConnection
{
    public void addAttributes(Search inSearch)
    {
        inSearch.setAttribute(
            "Google Last Check",
            new Date().toLocaleString());

        GoogleSearch search = new GoogleSearch();

        // Set mandatory attributes
        search.setKey(DeveloperTokens.googleKey);
        search.setQueryString(inSearch.getProductTitle());
```

Example 4-13. Google connectivity (continued)

```
        // Set optional attributes
        search.setSafeSearch(true);
        // Invoke the actual search
        GoogleSearchResult result = null;
        try
        {
            result = search.doSearch( );
        } catch (GoogleSearchFault e)
        {
            e.printStackTrace( );
        }
        // process the result

        if (result != null)
        {
            inSearch.setAttribute(
                "Google Number of Hits",
                Integer.toString(
                    result.getEstimatedTotalResultsCount( )));

            GoogleSearchResultElement[] mySearchElements =
                result.getResultElements( );

            for (int i = 0; i < mySearchElements.length; i++)
            {
                inSearch.setAttribute(
                    "Google Result " + i,
                    mySearchElements[i].toString( ));
                if (i > 4)
                {
                    i = mySearchElements.length;
                }
            }
        }
    }
  }
}
```

Developer Tokens

You may have noticed references to a DeveloperTokens class (e.g. DeveloperTokens. amazon_associates, or DeveloperTokens.amazon_token). This class is a single static class with a set of Strings containing the various developer tokens used throughout this chapter. The class shown in Example 4-14 contains only placeholder strings of the approximate correct length.

Example 4-14. Private developer tokens

```
package com.cascadetg.ch04;

public class DeveloperTokens
{
```

Example 4-14. Private developer tokens (continued)

```
    // Amazon userID token
    public static String amazon_token = "12345678901234";
    // Amazon assoicates ID
    public static String amazon_associates = "123456789-20";

    // eBay userID (the "visible" user identification, i.e. the buyer &
    // seller user.
    public static String eBay_userid = "1234567890";
    public static String ebay_userPassword = "1234567890";

    // devId, appId, certId as specified by the eBay Developer's
    // Program
    public static String ebay_devId = "12345678901234567890123456567890";
    public static String appId =      "12345678901234567890123456567890";
    public static String certId =     "12345678901234567890123456567890";

    // Google web services ID key
    public static String googleKey = "12345678901234567890123456789012";
}
```

As you've seen, actually making the connection to a provider isn't that hard (especially after creating bindings or utility classes to make it easier to access). Different vendors have different registration systems, pricing models, and different expectations in terms of security, but at least all offer free access to their system for developers to start building and testing applications, and all have published documentation and interfaces.

CHAPTER 5

Project 2: Auctions and Shipping

I've done some work with eBay, and so have a number of my friends and family. When you first start selling, it's usually an item or two, something small. Soon enough, selling things can become a fun side business. This in turn leads to a lot of time answering questions via email such as "how much will it cost to ship that to Florida?"

This chapter shows how to automate the process of posting auctions on eBay, and use the web services provided by FedEx to automatically include shipping estimates in the description of the auctions.

For this example, you'll build a command-line application that reads an XML file with details about the various auctions being posted. When the application successfully posts the auctions, it will note this information in the XML file and then write it back out to disk (avoiding duplicate posts).

Auction Listing XML

Start with a basic XML file format for writing auction posts. The goal here is to have a simple format a human can easily modify. This XML is shown in Example 5-1.

Example 5-1. Basic auctions XML

```
<?xml version="1.0" encoding="UTF-8"?>
<eBayAuctions>
   <Auction>
      <Category>37920</Category>
      <Weight>5.0</Weight>
      <MinimumBid>50</MinimumBid>
      <Title>Wonderful Ancient Chinese Basket</Title>
      <Description>This magnificent basket was handcrafted
by monks over one hundred years ago.</Description>
      <AuctionID>4500404174</AuctionID>
   </Auction>
   <Auction>
```

Example 5-1. Basic auctions XML (continued)

```
    <Category>2206</Category>
    <Weight>50.0</Weight>
    <MinimumBid>100</MinimumBid>
    <Title>Reproduction 1632 European World Map</Title>
    <Description><![CDATA[<b>Beautiful</b> cloth map of
the world as known to western Europe in 1632 - complete
with warnings about dragons!]]></Description>
    <AuctionID>4500404176</AuctionID>
  </Auction>
</eBayAuctions>
```

As shown in the example, this is a straightforward XML format. There are two auctions with the category, weight, minimum bid, title, and description specified. You don't want embedded HTML to be treated as part of the structure, so the description for the second auction is wrapped in the XML escape sequence:

```
    <![CDATA[ ... ]]>
```

As shown in Figure 5-1, you can do some simple validation of the XML file in a modern web browser, which allows you to easily ensure that the file is valid XML. You can even write a DTD or XML schema to validate the file, but for trivial purposes, this will suffice.

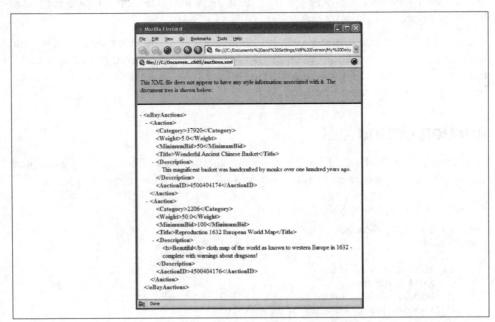

Figure 5-1. Viewing auctions.xml

Processing the Auction XML

Now that you've described your auctions using XML, you need to process that information and generate the posts. An example of the output of the program is shown in Example 5-2. As you can see from the output, the application will read an XML file, retrieve the FedEx shipping quote, and then post an auction listing on eBay.

Example 5-2. Output from auction listing

```
Starting to process ./com/cascadetg/ch05/auctions.xml
Getting FedEx quotes for Wonderful Ancient Chinese Basket...done.
Wonderful Ancient Chinese Basket [4500404259] has been listed.
Getting FedEx quotes for Reproduction 1632 European World Map...done.
Reproduction 1632 European World Map [4500404260] has been listed.
Changes complete. (18546 ms elapsed)
```

Figure 5-2 is a class diagram that illustrates the application structure we'll create in this chapter. There are three classes: an Auction class parses the XML and generates the listings, a FedExShipping class encapsulates the FedEx interactivity, and a FedExTokens class contains identification information (analogous to the username and password for the FedEx account).

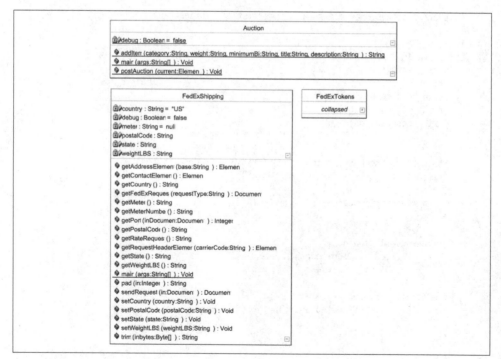

Figure 5-2. Auction listing classes

The class with main( ) is Auction; it expects an XML file to be passed as an argument, as shown in Example 5-3.

Example 5-3. Auction.java

```java
package com.cascadetg.ch05;

import java.io.FileOutputStream;

import org.jdom.input.SAXBuilder;
import org.jdom.output.XMLOutputter;
import org.jdom.*;

import com.cascadetg.ch04.EbayAPISimpleCall;

public class Auction
{
    static boolean debug = false;

    /**
     * Use this method to list an item. Most of these values are
     * self-explanatory, except for category. Categories are integers
     * defined on a per-region basis by eBay. For the US list, see
     *
     * http://listings.ebay.com/aw/listings/list/categories.html
     *
     */
    public static String addItem(
        String category,
        String weight,
        String minimumBid,
        String title,
        String description)
    {

        StringBuffer newDescription = new StringBuffer(description);
        if (!description.startsWith("<![CDATA["))
        {
            newDescription.insert(0, "<![CDATA[");
        } else
        {
            newDescription.delete(
                newDescription.length() - 3,
                newDescription.length());
        }
        newDescription.append(
            "<BR><BR><B>Estimated Shipping Fees...</B>");

        try
        {
            System.out.print(
                "Getting FedEx quotes for " + title + "...");
```

Example 5-3. Auction.java (continued)

```
        FedExShipping myShipper = new FedExShipping( );
        myShipper.setWeightLBS(weight);

        myShipper.setPostalCode("10002");
        myShipper.setState("NY");
        newDescription.append("<BR>New York, NY : US$");
        newDescription.append(myShipper.getRateRequest( ));

        myShipper.setPostalCode("96813");
        myShipper.setState("HI");
        newDescription.append("<BR>Honolulu, HI : US$");
        newDescription.append(myShipper.getRateRequest( ));

        myShipper.setPostalCode("94112");
        myShipper.setState("CA");
        newDescription.append("<BR>San Francisco, CA : US$");
        newDescription.append(myShipper.getRateRequest( ));

        newDescription.append("<BR><BR><B>Thanks for bidding!</B>");
        newDescription.append("]]>");
        System.out.println("done.");

    } catch (Exception e)
    {
        e.printStackTrace( );
        return null;

    }

    // Here, we use the same code as in Chapter 4 to
    // make the call to eBay. Note that we're passing in
    // the barest minimum arguments here to successfully
    // post an eBay auction - there is a *huge* list of
    // settings, including things like setting promotional
    // options (like listing with a bold title).
    EbayAPISimpleCall myCall = new EbayAPISimpleCall( );
    myCall.setApiVerb("AddItem");
    myCall.setArgument("Category", category);
    myCall.setArgument("CheckoutDetailsSpecified", "N");
    myCall.setArgument("Country", "US");
    myCall.setArgument("Currency", "1");
    myCall.setArgument("Description", newDescription.toString( ));
    myCall.setArgument("Duration", "7");
    myCall.setArgument(
        "Location",
        FedExTokens.fedExAddressCity
            + ", "
            + FedExTokens.fedExAddressState);
    myCall.setArgument("MinimumBid", minimumBid);
    myCall.setArgument("Quantity", "1");
    myCall.setArgument("Region", "0");
    myCall.setArgument("Title", title);
```

Example 5-3. Auction.java (continued)

```
        myCall.setArgument("VisaMaster", "1");
        myCall.setArgument("PersonalCheck", "1");

        // After setting the call up, here we actually connect
        // to the eBay server.
        org.jdom.Document myResults = myCall.executeCall();

        // Here we parse the XML returned by eBay, looking for
        // the Item ID and returning it if found.
        try
        {
            if (debug)
                new XMLOutputter().output(myResults, System.out);
            return myResults.getRootElement().getChild(
                "Item").getChildText(
                "Id");
        } catch (Exception e)
        {
            e.printStackTrace();
        }
        return null;
    }

    public static void postAuction(Element current)
    {
        // First, we check to see if the auction has been
        // listed before. If so, print this out and then
        // return.
        if (current.getChild("AuctionID") != null)
        {
            System.out.println(
                current.getChildText("Title")
                    + " ["
                    + current.getChildText("AuctionID")
                    + "] already listed.");
            return;
        }

        // We try to post the item with the needed values from
        // the XML.
        String id =
            addItem(
                current.getChildText("Category"),
                current.getChildText("Weight"),
                current.getChildText("MinimumBid"),
                current.getChildText("Title"),
                current.getChildText("Description"));

        // If id is null, there was some sort of problem.
        if (id == null)
        {
```

Example 5-3. Auction.java (continued)

```java
            System.out.println("Error with auction.");
            return;
        }

        // Ok, everything looks good. We attach the new eBay listing
        // ID number to the Auction as an AuctionID and we're done.
        Element newID = new Element("AuctionID");
        newID.setText(id);
        current.addContent(newID);
        System.out.println(
            current.getChildText("Title")
                + " ["
                + current.getChildText("AuctionID")
                + "] has been listed.");

    }

    public static void main(String[] args)
    {
        if (args == null)
        {
            System.out.println("Must pass a file name to continue.");
            return;
        }

        if (args.length == 0)
        {
            System.out.println("Must pass a file name to continue.");
            return;
        }

        System.out.println("Starting to process " + args[0]);
        long timing = System.currentTimeMillis();

        try
        {
            // Load the input file and process it as XML.
            java.io.File myFile = new java.io.File(args[0]);
            org.jdom.Document myDocument =
                new SAXBuilder().build(myFile);

            // Look at the XML and find all of the auctions
            myDocument.getRootElement();
            java.util.List myAuctions =
                myDocument.getRootElement().getChildren("Auction");

            // Loop through the resulting auction list and post each
            // one.
            for (int i = 0; i < myAuctions.size(); i++)
            {
                postAuction((Element)myAuctions.get(i));
            }
```

Example 5-3. Auction.java (continued)

```
        // We'll be saving the output to disk as XML again.
        // Here, we set up the output to be nicely formatted
        // for a human reader.
        XMLOutputter myOutput = new XMLOutputter( );
        myOutput.setOmitDeclaration(false);
        myOutput.setTextNormalize(true);
        myOutput.setNewlines(true);
        myOutput.setIndent("   ");

        // Flush the changes made (the new auction listings) to
        // disk. Auctions with an AuctionID will not be processed
        // again to prevent duplicate listings.
        FileOutputStream myFileOS = new FileOutputStream(myFile);
        myOutput.output(myDocument, myFileOS);

        // Calculate how long this took in milliseconds
        long elapsed = System.currentTimeMillis( ) - timing;
        System.out.println(
            "Changes complete. (" + elapsed + " ms elapsed)");

    } catch (Exception e)
    {
        System.out.println("Unable to process.");
        e.printStackTrace( );
    }

  }
}
```

The code shown in Example 5-3 accepts a single command-line argument: the name of the XML file (*auctions.xml*) described in Example 5-1. The Auction.main( ) method loops through looking for auctions, and calling addItem( ) and postItem( ) to post the data.

As shown in the postAuction( ) method, the relevant details are extracted from the XML. From there, the addItem( ) method connects to the FedEx server to retrieve three example destinations. Three default locales (New York, Hawaii, and California) are used to generate approximate shipping fees using the FedExShipping object. This data is then appended to the end of the auction description, and the EbayAPISimpleCall class originally described in Chapter 4 is used to post the auction to eBay.

The connectivity to the FedEx web service is wrapped using the FedExShipping class. We'll look at this interface in more detail, but let's start with a bit of an overview of the FedEx web services.

Connecting to FedEx

Sorting out the FedEx offerings can at first be a bit confusing. There are a variety of technologies, and it can be hard to understand which one is best to use. Indeed, it can be hard, when sorting through the FedEx web site, to figure out which package you should even download.

Start by visiting *http://www.fedex.com/us/solutions/wis/index.html/*. As shown in Figure 5-3, there are a variety of offerings, including the FedEx Ship Manager API, FedEx Ship Manager Direct, and XML Tools.

Go to the download page for the FedEx APIs. As of this writing, the URL is *https://www.fedex.com/cgi-bin/shipapiDownload.cgi?link=4&first=y*, but it may change. As shown in Figure 5-4, use FSM API for connections and XML Tools to actually send and retrieve data.

After registering and filling out the appropriate forms, you will be emailed instructions on how to download and install the SDK files. Of key interest is the main JAR file; if you downloaded and installed the SDK in the default location, you'll find this at *C:\Program Files\FedEx\FedEx Ship Manager API\java\lib\FedExAPI.JAR*. Make sure that the JAR file is on your class path.

The code shown in Example 5-4 shows how to actually connect to the FedEx server and retrieve the data. A utility `main( )` method is provided to test this functionality.

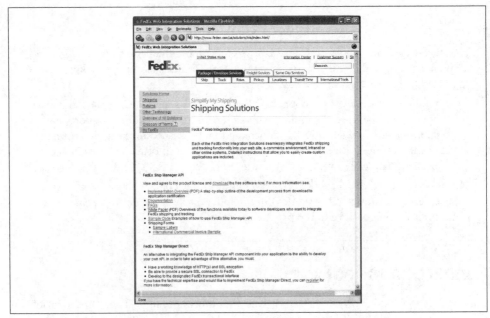

Figure 5-3. FedEx Solutions web site

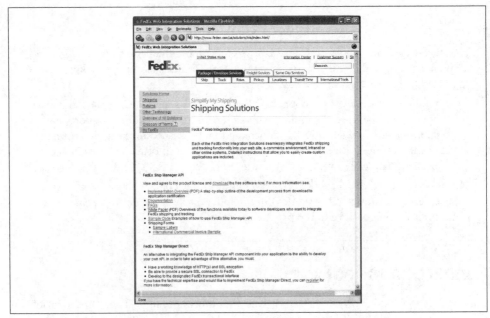

Figure 5-4. Choosing FedEx connectivity options

Example 5-4. FedExShipping.java

```java
package com.cascadetg.ch05;

import org.jdom.Document;
import org.jdom.Namespace;
import org.jdom.Element;
import org.jdom.input.SAXBuilder;
import org.jdom.output.XMLOutputter;

import com.fedex.api.*;

public class FedExShipping
{

    // We'll keep track of the meter id here.
    String meter = null;

    /**
     * Unfortunately, the FedExAPI sometimes returns garbage 0 bytes,
     * which need to be trimmed before the returned XML can be parsed.
     *
     * Therefore, we have this utility method that trims 0-value bytes
     * from an array of bytes.
     */
    public String trim(byte[] inbytes)
    {
        byte[] trimmed = null;
        for (int i = 0; i < inbytes.length; i++)
        {
            if (inbytes[i] == 0)
            {
                return new String(inbytes, 0, i);
            }
        }
        return new String(inbytes);
    }

    /**
     * @param carrierCode
     *              valid values are ALL, FDXE, FDXG, or null to not set.
     * @return
     */
    public Element getRequestHeaderElement(String carrierCode)
    {
        // Next, we create and add the RequestHeader element
        org.jdom.Element requestHeader =
            new org.jdom.Element("RequestHeader");

        // We'll be using this currentElement object to create
        // and set the various tags as needed.
        Element currentElement =
            new Element("CustomerTransactionIdentifier").addContent(
```

Example 5-4. FedExShipping.java (continued)

```
             new java.util.Date( ).toString( ));
    requestHeader.addContent((Element)currentElement.clone( ));

    currentElement.setName("AccountNumber");
    currentElement.setText(FedExTokens.fedExAccountNumber);
    requestHeader.addContent((Element)currentElement.clone( ));

    if (meter != null)
    {
        currentElement.setName("MeterNumber");
        currentElement.setText(meter);
        requestHeader.addContent((Element)currentElement.clone( ));
    }

    if (carrierCode != null)
    {
        currentElement.setName("CarrierCode");
        currentElement.setText(carrierCode);
        requestHeader.addContent((Element)currentElement.clone( ));

    }

    return requestHeader;
}

public Element getContactElement( )
{
    // After setting the RequestHeader elements, we next need to
    // set the Contact element
    Element contactElement = new Element("Contact");

    Element currentElement = new Element("PersonName");
    currentElement.setText(FedExTokens.fedExPersonName);
    contactElement.addContent((Element)currentElement.clone( ));

    currentElement.setName("CompanyName");
    currentElement.setText(FedExTokens.fedExCompanyName);
    contactElement.addContent((Element)currentElement.clone( ));

    currentElement.setName("Department");
    currentElement.setText(FedExTokens.fedExDepartment);
    contactElement.addContent((Element)currentElement.clone( ));

    currentElement.setName("PhoneNumber");
    currentElement.setText(FedExTokens.fedExPhoneNumber);
    contactElement.addContent((Element)currentElement.clone( ));

    currentElement.setName("E-MailAddress");
    currentElement.setText(FedExTokens.fedExEmail);
    contactElement.addContent((Element)currentElement.clone( ));

    return contactElement;
```

Example 5-4. FedExShipping.java (continued)

```java
    }

    public Element getAddressElement(String base)
    {
        // Next, we set the Address element.
        Element addressElement = new Element(base);

        Element currentElement = new Element("Line1");
        currentElement.setText(FedExTokens.fedExAddressLine1);
        addressElement.addContent((Element)currentElement.clone());

        currentElement.setName("Line2");
        currentElement.setText(FedExTokens.fedExAddressLine2);
        addressElement.addContent((Element)currentElement.clone());

        currentElement.setName("City");
        currentElement.setText(FedExTokens.fedExAddressCity);
        addressElement.addContent((Element)currentElement.clone());

        currentElement.setName("StateOrProvinceCode");
        currentElement.setText(FedExTokens.fedExAddressState);
        addressElement.addContent((Element)currentElement.clone());

        currentElement.setName("PostalCode");
        currentElement.setText(FedExTokens.fedExAddressZIP);
        addressElement.addContent((Element)currentElement.clone());

        currentElement.setName("CountryCode");
        currentElement.setText(FedExTokens.fedExCountry);
        addressElement.addContent((Element)currentElement.clone());

        return addressElement;
    }

    public Document getFedExRequest(String requestType)
    {
        // First, we create a new XML document and set the
        // namespaces as requested by FedEx.
        Document message = new org.jdom.Document( );
        message.setRootElement(new org.jdom.Element(requestType));

        Namespace api =
            Namespace.getNamespace(
                "api",
                "http://www.fedex.com/fsmapi");

        Namespace xsi =
            Namespace.getNamespace(
                "xsi",
                "http://www.w3.org/2001/XMLSchema-instance");
```

Example 5-4. FedExShipping.java (continued)

```java
        message.getRootElement().addNamespaceDeclaration(api);
        message.getRootElement().addNamespaceDeclaration(xsi);

        message.getRootElement().setAttribute(
            "noNamespaceSchemaLocation",
            requestType + ".xsd",
            Namespace.getNamespace(
                "xsi",
                "http://www.w3.org/2001/XMLSchema-instance"));

        return message;
    }

    public String pad(int in)
    {
        if (in > 9)
            return new String(Integer.toString(in));
        return new String("0" + in);

    }

    String weightLBS;
    String postalCode;
    String state;
    String country = "US";

    /**
     * Used to retrieve a rate request from the FedEx server. Note that
     * this takes on average about two seconds by my highly informal
     * estimate, plus an additional three seconds the first time you
     * look up your meter number (so the first time you make this call
     * it could easily take over five seconds to return!)
     */

    public String getRateRequest()
    {
        if (meter == null)
            if (debug)
            {
                System.out.println("Meter #: " + getMeterNumber());
            } else
            {
                getMeterNumber();
            }

        Document myMessage = getFedExRequest("FDXRateRequest");
        myMessage.getRootElement().addContent(
            getRequestHeaderElement("FDXG"));

        Element currentElement = new Element("ShipDate");
        java.util.Date today = new java.util.Date();
        currentElement.setText(
```

Example 5-4. FedExShipping.java (continued)

```
            (today.getYear( ) + 1900)
                + "-"
                + pad(today.getMonth( ))
                + "-"
                + pad(today.getDate( )));
    myMessage.getRootElement( ).addContent(
        (Element)currentElement.clone( ));

    currentElement.setName("DropoffType");
    currentElement.setText("REGULARPICKUP");
    myMessage.getRootElement( ).addContent(
        (Element)currentElement.clone( ));

    currentElement.setName("Service");
    currentElement.setText("FEDEXGROUND");
    myMessage.getRootElement( ).addContent(
        (Element)currentElement.clone( ));

    currentElement.setName("Packaging");
    currentElement.setText("FEDEXBOX");
    myMessage.getRootElement( ).addContent(
        (Element)currentElement.clone( ));

    currentElement.setName("WeightUnits");
    currentElement.setText("LBS");
    myMessage.getRootElement( ).addContent(
        (Element)currentElement.clone( ));

    currentElement.setName("Weight");
    currentElement.setText(weightLBS);
    myMessage.getRootElement( ).addContent(
        (Element)currentElement.clone( ));

    Element origin = new Element("OriginAddress");

    currentElement.setName("StateOrProvinceCode");
    currentElement.setText(FedExTokens.fedExAddressState);
    origin.addContent((Element)currentElement.clone( ));

    currentElement.setName("PostalCode");
    currentElement.setText(FedExTokens.fedExAddressZIP);
    origin.addContent((Element)currentElement.clone( ));

    currentElement.setName("CountryCode");
    currentElement.setText(FedExTokens.fedExCountry);
    origin.addContent((Element)currentElement.clone( ));
    myMessage.getRootElement( ).addContent(origin);

    Element destination = new Element("DestinationAddress");
```

Example 5-4. FedExShipping.java (continued)

```java
        currentElement.setName("StateOrProvinceCode");
        currentElement.setText(state);
        destination.addContent((Element)currentElement.clone());

        currentElement.setName("PostalCode");
        currentElement.setText(postalCode);
        destination.addContent((Element)currentElement.clone());

        currentElement.setName("CountryCode");
        currentElement.setText(country);
        destination.addContent((Element)currentElement.clone());
        myMessage.getRootElement().addContent(destination);

        Element payment = new Element("Payment");
        currentElement.setName("PayorType");
        currentElement.setText("SENDER");
        payment.addContent((Element)currentElement.clone());
        myMessage.getRootElement().addContent(payment);

        currentElement.setName("PackageCount");
        currentElement.setText("1");
        myMessage.getRootElement().addContent(
            (Element)currentElement.clone());

        try
        {
            if (debug)
                new XMLOutputter().output(myMessage, System.out);

            org.jdom.Document reply = sendRequest(myMessage);

            if (debug)
                new XMLOutputter().output(reply, System.out);

            return reply
                .getRootElement()
                .getChild("EstimatedCharges")
                .getChild("ListCharges")
                .getChildText("NetCharge");

        } catch (Exception e)
        {
            e.printStackTrace();
        }

        return null;
    }

    /**
     * This class relies heavily on the values supplied in the
     * FedExTokens class for the data to be sent. Note that FedEx
     * performs validation on the data sent to the server, so you need
```

Example 5-4. FedExShipping.java (continued)

```java
     * to make sure that you're sending over valid information (e.g. a
     * valid ZIP code).
     *
     * Note that there is no reason not to cache the meter number -
     * indeed, if you intend to use the FedEx API heavily, you ought to
     * just enter the meter number as a static value in your
     * FedExTokens equivalent.
     */
    public String getMeterNumber( )
    {
        String finalResponse = null;

        Document myMessage = getFedExRequest("FDXSubscriptionRequest");

        myMessage.getRootElement( ).addContent(
            getRequestHeaderElement(null));

        myMessage.getRootElement( ).addContent(getContactElement( ));

        myMessage.getRootElement( ).addContent(
            getAddressElement("Address"));

        org.jdom.Document myReply = sendRequest(myMessage);

        try
        {
            if (myReply.getRootElement( ).getChild("MeterNumber")
                == null)
            {
                System.out.println("Unable to find meter number:");
                new XMLOutputter( ).output(myReply, System.out);
            }
            finalResponse =
                myReply.getRootElement( ).getChildText("MeterNumber");
            meter = finalResponse;
            return finalResponse;
        } catch (Exception e)
        {
            e.printStackTrace( );
            try
            {
                new XMLOutputter( ).output(myReply, System.out);
            } catch (Exception e1)
            {
                e1.printStackTrace( );
            }

        }
        return null;

    }
```

Example 5-4. FedExShipping.java (continued)

```java
public boolean debug = false;

public int getPort(org.jdom.Document inDocument)
{
    String rootElement = inDocument.getRootElement( ).getName( );
    if (rootElement.compareTo("FDXRateRequest") == 0)
        return 2518;
    if (rootElement.compareTo("FDXSubscriptionRequest") == 0)
        return 2523;

    return -1;
}

public org.jdom.Document sendRequest(org.jdom.Document in)
{
    try
    {
        XMLOutputter myOutputter = new XMLOutputter( );
        myOutputter.setOmitDeclaration(false);

        if (debug)
            myOutputter.output(in, System.out);

        byte[] response = new byte[0];

        byte[] request;

        request =
            myOutputter.outputString(in).toString( ).getBytes(
                "UTF8");

        if (debug)
            System.out.println("Sending transaction...");

        response =
            FedExAPI.transact(
                getPort(in),
                request,
                "127.0.0.1",
                8190,
                125);

        org.jdom.Document myReply =
            new SAXBuilder( ).build(
                new java.io.StringReader(trim(response)));

        return myReply;

    } catch (Exception e)
    {
        e.printStackTrace( );
```

Example 5-4. FedExShipping.java (continued)

```java
        }
        return null;
    }

    public static void main(String[] args)
    {
        boolean debug = false;
        if (args != null)
            if (args.length > 0)
                if (args[0].compareTo("debug") == 0)
                    debug = true;

        FedExShipping myShipper = new FedExShipping();

        long timing = System.currentTimeMillis();
        long elapsed = System.currentTimeMillis() - timing;

        System.out.println("Elapsed: " + elapsed);
        timing = System.currentTimeMillis();

        myShipper.setWeightLBS("10.0");

        myShipper.setPostalCode("10002");
        myShipper.setState("NY");

        System.out.println(
            "New York Rate request: " + myShipper.getRateRequest());
        elapsed = System.currentTimeMillis() - timing;
        System.out.println("Elapsed: " + elapsed);
        timing = System.currentTimeMillis();

        myShipper.setPostalCode("96813");
        myShipper.setState("HI");
        System.out.println(
            "Hawaii Rate request: " + myShipper.getRateRequest());
        elapsed = System.currentTimeMillis() - timing;
        System.out.println("Elapsed: " + elapsed);
        timing = System.currentTimeMillis();

        myShipper.setPostalCode("98121");
        myShipper.setState("WA");
        System.out.println(
            "Seattle, WA Rate request: " + myShipper.getRateRequest());
        elapsed = System.currentTimeMillis() - timing;
        System.out.println("Elapsed: " + elapsed);
        timing = System.currentTimeMillis();

    }

    public String getCountry()
    {
```

Example 5-4. FedExShipping.java (continued)

```
        return country;
    }

  public void setCountry(String country)
  {
        this.country = country;
  }

    public String getPostalCode( )
    {
        return postalCode;
    }

    public void setPostalCode(String postalCode)
    {
        this.postalCode = postalCode;
    }

    public String getState( )
    {
        return state;
    }

    public void setState(String state)
    {
        this.state = state;
    }

    public String getWeightLBS( )
    {
        return weightLBS;
    }

    public void setWeightLBS(String weightLBS)
    {
        this.weightLBS = weightLBS;
}

        public String getMeter( )
{
  return meter;
 }
 }
```

The code in Example 5-4 performs two tasks: first, given your FedEx registration, it gets your meter number. Second, given some additional specific information (weight, state, postal code, and country), it returns a rate estimate for a package. Your meter number is the FedEx number used to track your account and is required by most FedEx operations.

Note that there is a lot of XML document processing that goes on in Example 5-4. The FedEx XML format is heavily hierarchical, requiring subnodes to be attached to nodes. For readability, the code to set up a single transaction is broken into several chunks (getRequestHeaderElement( ), getContactElement( ), getAddressElement( )), but it's still a heavily complex process of processing FedEx-specific XML. A full description of the various XML commands supported by FedEx can be found at *http://www.fedex.com/us/solutions/wis/pdf/xml_transguide.pdf?link=4*. The complexity arises not from any particularly complex algorithm, but rather the sheer number of options and the complexity of the XML hierarchy.

What Are the Other FedEx Choices?

You'll notice that there are two other choices: *FSM Direct* for connectivity and *FedEx Tagged Transaction* for the data format.

FSM Direct allows you to connect directly to the FedEx systems using HTTPS, similar to the method used to connect to eBay. Fortunately, the FSM API takes care of all this connectivity automatically; the provided JAR file handles the connectivity. If for some reason you wish to manually control the connectivity via HTTPS, you may wish to investigate FSM Direct.

FedEx Tagged Transactions are an alternative to the XML format that FedEx uses (called XML Tools). It's a pre-XML format, based on special ASCII formatting. Here's an example of a FedEx Tagged Transaction:

```
2016:0,"021"4,"Total Widget Rebuilders"5,"445 East
Street"7,"Dallas"8,"TX"9,"75247"10,"123456789"498,"123567"117,"US"183,"21455587
65"50,"US"11,"ABC Widget" 12,"Bernard F. Smith"13,"322 Latta Woods"14,"Suite
26"15,"Roanoke"16,"VA"17,"24012"18,"7035551212"23,"1"1401,"4.
0"1273,"03"1274,"03"25,"SPECIAL CALL-IN"24,
"20000103"51,"Y"1115,"130555"1368,"1"1369,"1"1370,"5"1116,"I"75,"LBS"3025,"FDXE
"1333,"1"99,""
```

Using the XML format, you avoid having to worry about parsing this data format.

Even though there is a lot of code in Example 5-4, it's the bare minimum to actually get a rate request from FedEx. There are a significant number of additional options that can be set to obtain much more precise rate quotes. For applications using this class, however, all this is abstracted into an ordinary Java class with a few set...( ) methods and a getRateRequest( ) actually retrieving the data. Similarly, the remaining FedEx XML web service methods could be bound to Java classes.

A single class, shown in Example 5-5, stores the important information about your account.

Even if you compile this data into a *.class* or *.jar*, and even if you run most obfuscators, it's still very easy to retrieve the information using a decompiler. You should consider this class, even compiled, to be equivalent to a password file!

This example doesn't contain real values, but the length and format of the strings are correct. You'll want to enter your own information here, as provided by FedEx, instead of using the values shown.

Example 5-5. FedExTokens.java

```java
package com.cascadetg.ch05;

public class FedExTokens
{

    public static String fedExAccountNumber = "123456789";
    public static String fedExPersonName = "Will Iverson";
    public static String fedExCompanyName = "Cascade Technology Group";
    public static String fedExDepartment = "Shipping";
    public static String fedExPhoneNumber = "5105551212";
    public static String fedExEmail = "fedex@yourdomain.com";

    public static String fedExAddressLine1 = "123 Anywhere Ave";
    public static String fedExAddressLine2 = "Suite 101";
    public static String fedExAddressCity = "Universal City";
    public static String fedExAddressState = "CA";
    public static String fedExAddressZIP = "95111";
    public static String fedExCountry = "US";

}
```

In this chapter, you used two different web services to provide an easier environment for both the seller and the buyer. The seller can automate a boring task, and the buyer can get an idea of the true cost of an auction while browsing through the auction listings (avoiding rude surprises). It's easy to imagine extending this application to do many more things, such as monitor the current status of posted auctions or generate reports.

CHAPTER 6

Project 3: Billing and Faxing

If you manage to successfully sell any quantity of items on the Internet, it's hard to imagine not setting up automated systems to help handle the workload. You see this sort of automation all of the time; for example, you expect an automated system to automatically send a confirmation email when an order has been placed. Upon occasion, however, you may not be fortunate enough to work with individuals that have access to the latest technologies, such as email and the Web (yes, for some people those are the latest technologies). For example, your manufacturing partner may not be up to speed. Even in those situations, you can probably still rely on that old standby—the fax.

This chapter shows how to set up a system whereby you receive a payment notification from PayPal and respond by sending a fax containing the order information. PayPal is the well-known payment processing service, *http://www.paypal.com/* (see Figure 6-1). For faxes, we'll be using the web services provided by InterFAX, *http://www.interfax.net/* (shown in Figure 6-2).

PayPal's development offerings are all listed on the main page, but the specific technology we're interested in here is Instant Payment Notification (IPN), *http://www.paypal.com/cgi-bin/webscr?cmd=p/xcl/rec/ipn-intro-outside*. The idea is fairly straightforward: when a PayPal payment is received, the PayPal server sends a notification to a URL you specify. There is no specific developer sign up required to make use of the IPN functionality; you just use the standard PayPal account registration.

The fax services provided by InterFAX allow you to send faxes using any of a variety of technologies; in addition to SOAP, you can also use email. A free developer registration (*http://www.interfax.net/en/dev/index.html*) allows you to send test faxes to a single designated phone number for free (up to a $10 credit, which can be refreshed for free on request).

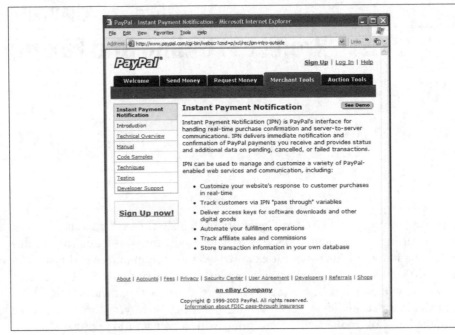

Figure 6-1. PayPal instant payment notification web site

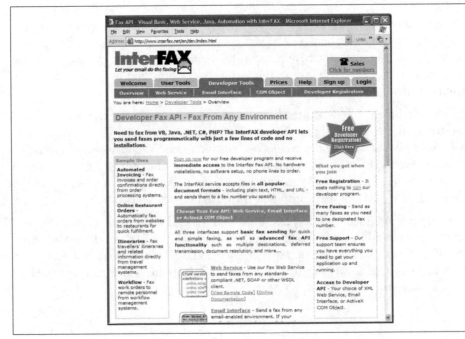

Figure 6-2. InterFAX developer site

Starting the Transaction

To kick off our example, let's start with a simple HTML page that will initiate our transaction, as shown in Figure 6-3.

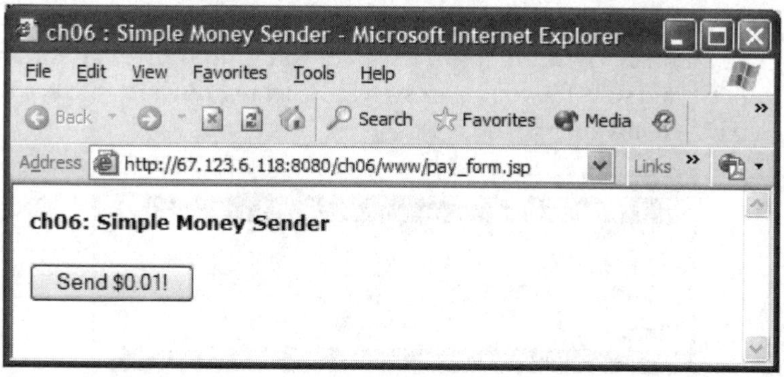

Figure 6-3. Initial payment screen

It's not the world's most sophisticated marketing page, but it does the job and is easy to understand. The HTML for this simple page is shown in Example 6-1.

Example 6-1. Payment initialization form

```
<%@ page contentType="text/html; charset=iso-8859-1"
language="java" import="com.cascadetg.ch06.*" %>
<HTML>
<HEAD><title>ch06 : Simple Money Sender</title>
<link href="../../ch04/www/default.css"
rel="stylesheet" type="text/css">
</HEAD>
<BODY>
    <form action="https://www.paypal.com/cgi-bin/webscr" method="post">
      <p><strong>ch06: Simple Money Sender</strong></p>
      <p>
     <input type="hidden" name="cmd" value="_xclick">
     <input type="hidden" name="business"
     value="test_account@cascadetg.com">
     <input type="hidden" name="item_name" value="IPN Test">
     <input type="hidden" name="amount" value="0.01">
     <input type="hidden" name="return"
     value="http://67.123.6.118:8080/ch06/www/pay_form.jsp">
     <input type="hidden" name="notify_url"
     value="http://67.123.6.118:8080/ch06/www/notification.jsp">
     <!-- Note: The notify_url field is not required if the IPN
     URL was set in your account profile)-->
     <input type="submit" name="submit" value="Send $0.01!">
      </p>
```

Example 6-1. Payment initialization form (continued)

```
    </form>
</BODY>
</HTML>
```

Notice that the form is posted to the PayPal server, but `return` and `notify_url` form elements are used to point back to this server. The IP address shown, `67.123.6.118:8080`, is the WAN IP address and port for my server; you'll need to establish an Internet accessible address and port for your own system. Clicking the button takes the user to the PayPal server, as shown in Figure 6-4.

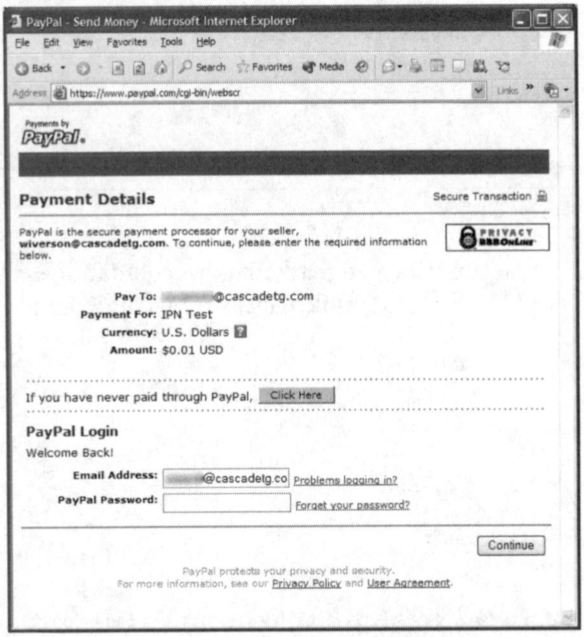

Figure 6-4. Initiating the PayPal transaction

Once at the PayPal server, users can walk through the rest of the transaction using the PayPal service, including entering credit card information and shipping address. When the order is complete, they are returned to the original *pay_form.jsp* page, ready to send another $0.01.

The example uses a transaction of $0.01 for this; it isn't a transaction you'd ever use PayPal for because PayPal and credit card company fees will absorb the penny. You can use PayPal's management services to refund the quantities sent, which is especially important if you need to test sending larger monetary sums.

As an additional feature, the example in this chapter generates faxes when a refund is sent. If an order is cancelled, you'll probably want to let your (fictional) business partner know as soon as possible.

Getting a Transaction Notification

When an order is processed, PayPal generates a notification that is then posted to the URL specified in the form as the hidden field notify_url. This is an example of a web service that relies on ordinary HTTP—no fancy SOAP or other RPC underpinnings.

Using a simple HTTP request/response is perhaps the most basic, universal real world web service. It works with virtually every programming language and requires no special configuration to use. It's a classic case of the simple solution being the best solution.

Example 6-2 shows the JSP used to receive notifications from the PayPal server.

Example 6-2. Notification JSP

```
<%@ page contentType="text/html; charset=iso-8859-1"
language="java" import="com.cascadetg.ch06.*" %>
<!DOCTYPE html PUBLIC "-//W3C//DTD XHTML 1.0 Transitional//EN" "http://www.w3.org/TR/
xhtml1/DTD/xhtml1-transitional.dtd">
<%
new PayPalReciept().handleRequest(request, response);
response.setStatus(200);
%>
```

The line response.setStatus(200) notifies PayPal that the notification has successfully been handled. By default, PayPal resends the notification until it gets a status code of 200 back, indicating that the transmission was successful. Disabling this line or substituting a different response code is an easy way to generate additional test load for your server without having to manually enter a lot of transactions.

The bulk of the work for this application is handled by supporting Java classes, as shown in Figure 6-5.

The first class, shown in Example 6-3, exposes one main method, handleRequest(), to the JSP page. In the handleRequest() method, the first thing to be done is verify that the data sent by PayPal is correct with the verifyRequest() method. The verifyRequest() method retrieves the parameters sent by PayPal and then posts

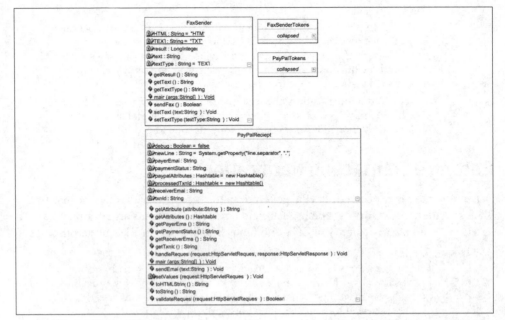

Figure 6-5. PayPal and Fax classes

them back to PayPal via an HTTPS connection, with an additional parameter added (cmd=_notify-validate).

Example 6-3. A PayPal receipt

```java
package com.cascadetg.ch06;

import java.util.*;
import java.net.*;
import java.io.*;

import javax.servlet.http.*;
import javax.mail.*;
import javax.mail.internet.*;

public class PayPalReciept
{
    // Used to store retrieved values from the PayPal submission.
    String paymentStatus;
    String txnId;
    String receiverEmail;
    String payerEmail;

    private static final boolean debug = false;

    // System.getProperty line to get the proper new line character[s].
    String newLine = System.getProperty("line.separator", ".");
```

Example 6-3. A PayPal receipt (continued)

```java
        // Keep track of sent transactions. Note that this is in-memory
        // storage only - for a "real" system you would want to persist
        // this information, as well as the rest of fields of this object.
        // (mostly likely to a database of some sort).
        private static Hashtable processedTxnId = new Hashtable();

        // This method takes an incoming request and validates it both
        // against the PayPal server and some internal logic.
        public boolean validateRequest(HttpServletRequest request)
        {
            try
            {
                // Read the post from PayPal system.
                Enumeration parameters = request.getParameterNames();
                // We then add a "cmd" attribute to send back to PayPal
                // to indicate that we want to validate the request.
                StringBuffer send =
                    new StringBuffer("cmd=_notify-validate");

                // Here, we put all of the parameters passed in from the
                // PayPal notification POST.
                while (parameters.hasMoreElements())
                {
                    String paramName = (String)parameters.nextElement();
                    String paramValue = request.getParameter(paramName);
                    send.append("&");
                    send.append(paramName);
                    send.append("=");
                    send.append(URLEncoder.encode(paramValue));
                }

                if (debug)
                    System.out.println(send.toString());

                // This next sequence opens a connection to the PayPal
                // server, sets up the connection, and writes the sent
                // parameters back to the PayPal server.
                URL paypalServer =
                    new URL("https://www.paypal.com/cgi-bin/webscr");
                URLConnection paypalConnection =
                    paypalServer.openConnection();
                paypalConnection.setDoOutput(true);
                paypalConnection.setRequestProperty(
                    "Content-Type",
                    "application/x-www-form-urlencoded");
                PrintWriter paypalServerWriter =
                    new PrintWriter(paypalConnection.getOutputStream());
                paypalServerWriter.println(send);
                paypalServerWriter.close();

                if (debug)
                    System.out.println("Sent to PayPal server.");
```

Example 6-3. A PayPal receipt (continued)

```
// We then need to read the response from the PayPal
// server.
BufferedReader in =
    new BufferedReader(
        new InputStreamReader(
            paypalConnection.getInputStream( )));
String paypalResponse = in.readLine( );
in.close( );

if (debug)
    System.out.println(
        "Read PayPal server response = " + paypalResponse);

// Set the values of this object from the values sent
// by the initial request. If these values are verified,
// we'll want them for later. If the values aren't
// verified, or something else is wrong, we'll want
// to track them for logging purposes.
setValues(request);

// If everything is ok, the response back should be
// VERIFIED. Otherwise, something went wrong.
if (paypalResponse.equals("VERIFIED"))
{
    // If it isn't completed, it's a status message of
    // some sort. We're only interested in Completed
    // payments.
    if (!paymentStatus.equals("Completed"))
        return false;

    // Make sure that we are the actual recipients of
    // the money.
    if (receiverEmail
        .compareToIgnoreCase(PayPalTokens.paypalEmail)
        != 0)
        return false;

    // Check the in-memory cache to verify that we
    // haven't already handled this transaction.
    if (processedTxnId.get(this.getTxnId( )) != null)
        return false;

    // Everything looks good, so let's add this to the
    // transaction cache.
    processedTxnId.put(this.getTxnId( ), this.getTxnId( ));

    return true;
} else
{
    System.out.println("Invalid PayPal transaction!");
    System.out.println(this.toString( ));
    return false;
```

Example 6-3. A PayPal receipt (continued)

```
            }
        } catch (Exception e)
        {
            System.out.println("Unable to connect to PayPal server.");
            e.printStackTrace( );
            return false;
        }
    }

    // "Flatten" the object to a String.
    public String toString( )
    {
        StringBuffer output = new StringBuffer( );
        Enumeration outEnum = this.getAttributes( ).keys( );

        while (outEnum.hasMoreElements( ))
        {
            String outputStr = (String)outEnum.nextElement( );
            output.append(outputStr);
            output.append(" : ");
            output.append(paypalAttributes.get(outputStr).toString( ));
            output.append(newLine);
        }

        return output.toString( );
    }

    public String toHTMLString( )
    {
        StringBuffer htmlString = new StringBuffer( );
        htmlString.append("<HTML><BODY>");
        htmlString.append("<TABLE HEIGHT='100%' WIDTH='100%'>");
        htmlString.append("<TR><TD>");

        Enumeration myValues = this.getAttributes( ).keys( );
        while (myValues.hasMoreElements( ))
        {
            String next = (String)myValues.nextElement( );
            htmlString.append(next);
            htmlString.append(" : ");
            htmlString.append(this.getAttribute(next).toString( ));
            htmlString.append("<BR>");
            htmlString.append(newLine);
        }

        htmlString.append("</TD></TR></TABLE></BODY></HTML>");
        return htmlString.toString( );

    }

    // PayPal can send a variety of attributes back as part of a
    // transaction. We're interested in all of them, so we'll note
    // them all.
```

Example 6-3. A PayPal receipt (continued)

```
Hashtable paypalAttributes = new Hashtable( );

public String getAttribute(String attribute)
{
    return (String)paypalAttributes.get((String)attribute);
}

public Hashtable getAttributes( )
{
    return paypalAttributes;
}

/**
 * Reads the incoming values and fills out the object. Notice that
 * we are also recording the incoming IP address - if someone is
 * sending fake requests, the IP address can be an important bit of
 * information.
 *
 * @param request
 */
private void setValues(HttpServletRequest request)
{
    paypalAttributes = new Hashtable(request.getParameterMap( ));
    Enumeration attributes = request.getParameterNames( );
    while (attributes.hasMoreElements( ))
    {
        String temp = (String)attributes.nextElement( );
        paypalAttributes.put(temp, request.getParameter(temp));
    }

    paypalAttributes.put(
        "incoming_ip",
        request.getRemoteAddr( ).toString( ));

    paymentStatus = request.getParameter("payment_status");
    txnId = request.getParameter("txn_id");
    receiverEmail = request.getParameter("receiver_email");
    payerEmail = request.getParameter("payer_email");
}

/**
 * The main entry point from the JSP page request. We'll look at
 * the request and validate it, and depending on the results, we'll
 * either send a notification email OR a fax and a notification
 * email.
 */
public void handleRequest(
    HttpServletRequest request,
    HttpServletResponse response)
{
    if (validateRequest(request))
    {
```

Example 6-3. A PayPal receipt (continued)

```
        if (debug)
            System.out.print("Sending fax... " + this.toString());
        FaxSender myFaxSender = new FaxSender();
        myFaxSender.setText(this.toHTMLString());
        myFaxSender.setTextType(FaxSender.HTML);
        if (debug)
            System.out.print("fax prepped...");
        myFaxSender.sendFax();
        this.paypalAttributes.put(
            "fax_id",
            myFaxSender.getResult().toString());

        if (debug)
            System.out.println("Fax sent.");

    }


    sendEmail(this.toString());
}

// These are the usual retrieval methods a'la the JavaBean
// patterns. Notice that there are only retrieval methods - no
// setters are provided.

public String getPayerEmail()
{
    return payerEmail;
}

public String getPaymentStatus()
{
    return paymentStatus;
}

public String getReceiverEmail()
{
    return receiverEmail;
}

/** Returns the transaction ID (aka TxnId) */
public String getTxnId()
{
    return txnId;
}

public void sendEmail(String text)
{
    try
    {
        java.util.Properties myProperties = new Properties();
        myProperties.put("mail.smtp.host", PayPalTokens.mailhost);
        myProperties.put("mail.smtp.auth", "true");
```

Example 6-3. A PayPal receipt (continued)

```
        Session mySession = Session.getInstance(myProperties);
        //mySession.setDebug(true);

        Transport myTransport = mySession.getTransport("smtp");
        myTransport.connect(
            PayPalTokens.mailhost,
            PayPalTokens.mailhost_username,
            PayPalTokens.mailhost_password);

        Message myMessage =
            new javax.mail.internet.MimeMessage(mySession);
        myMessage.setFrom(
            new InternetAddress(
                PayPalTokens.paypalEmail,
                "PayPal Listener"));
        myMessage.addRecipient(
            Message.RecipientType.TO,
            new InternetAddress(PayPalTokens.paypalEmail));
        myMessage.setSubject("PayPal Notification");
        myMessage.setContent(this.toHTMLString( ), "text/html");
        Address[] temp =
            { new InternetAddress(PayPalTokens.paypalEmail)};
        myMessage.setReplyTo(temp);
        myMessage.saveChanges( );

        myTransport.sendMessage(
            myMessage,
            myMessage.getAllRecipients( ));

        myTransport.close( );
    } catch (Exception e)
    {
        e.printStackTrace( );
    }
}

public static void main(String[] args)
{
    (new PayPalReciept( )).sendEmail("test");
}

}
```

If PayPal doesn't respond with a VERIFIED token, it's possible that someone is attempting to forge a transaction. If you see this occur in a real world environment, you should take immediate, aggressive steps to deal with this; it may be an attempt by a hacker to steal funds or even your identity.

Responding to the Transaction

Assuming the PayPal data is validated, a fax and an email are sent. If the data isn't validated, just an email is sent (helpful for immediate notification of a potential hacker). The email processing is handled using the standard JavaMail API (*http://java.sun.com/products/javamail/*).

 To recap, an unencrypted HTML form from a local server starts the transaction. This form specified an unencrypted notification URL for the receipt of the data (although an HTTPS connection can be used instead). Therefore, the HTTPS connection back to PayPal to validate this is pretty important; otherwise, the application might be getting a fake order that just happens to look like a PayPal request.

An example email, formatted as HTML is shown in Figure 6-6.

From: "PayPal Listener" <■■■■@cascadetg.com>
To: ■■■■@cascadetg.com
Subject: PayPal Notification

```
address_owner : 1
notify_version : 1.5
address_zip : ■■■■
payment_fee : 0.01
mc_fee : 0.01
address_state : CA
receiver id : ■■■■
fax_id : ■■■■
quantity : 1
address_status : confirmed
payer_email : ■■■■
txn_id : ■■■■
verify_sign : ■■■■
address_street : ■■■■
incoming_ip : 64.4.241.140
payment_type : instant
mc_currency : USD
last_name : ■■■■
payment_date : 20:29:50 Jan 04, 2004 PST
txn_type : web_accept
paypal_address_id : ■■■■
address_name : ■■■■
address_country : United States
ebay_address_id :
custom :
mc_gross : 0.01
payment_status : Completed
item_number :
address_city : ■■■■
payer_id : ■■■■
receiver_email : ■■■■@cascadetg.com
first_name : ■■■■
tax : 0.00
payer_status : unverified
business : ■■■■@cascadetg.com
payment_gross : 0.01
item_name : IPN Test
```

Figure 6-6. Email notification

It's easy to imagine adding additional logic to the PayPalReciept.toHTMLString() method for a more appealing and easier to understand design, but it contains all of the needed information.

The fax sending is encapsulated in a simple Java class, as shown in Example 6-4.

Example 6-4. Fax sender code

```
package com.cascadetg.ch06;

import cc.interfax.www.*;
import java.net.URL;
import org.apache.axis.client.*;
import javax.xml.namespace.QName;

/**
 * http://www.interfax.net/en/dev.html
 *
 * C:\devenv\axis-1_1\lib>java -classpath
 * commons-logging.jar;log4j-1.2.8.jar;wsdl4j.jar;axis.jar;
   commons-discovery.jar;jax
 * rpc.jar;saaj.jar org.apache.axis.wsdl.WSDL2Java
 * http://ws.interfax.net/dfs.asmx?wsdl
 */

public class FaxSender
{

    public static final String TEXT = "TXT";
    public static final String HTML = "HTM";

    String text;
    String textType = TEXT;

    long result;

    /**
     * This is the main method used to send a Fax. You'll want to set
     * the text to be sent and the text type before calling this.
     *
     * @return true if successful, false if not.
     */
    public boolean sendFax()
    {
        try
        {

            // Create an instance of the Web Service Object
            InterFaxSoapStub ifs =
                new InterFaxSoapStub(
                    new URL("http://ws.interfax.net/DFS.asmx"),
                    new Service(new QName("SendCharFax")));

            // Invoke the SendCharFax method
            result =
                ifs.sendCharFax(
                    FaxSenderTokens.faxUsername,
                    FaxSenderTokens.faxPassword,
                    FaxSenderTokens.faxTestFaxNumber,
```

Example 6-4. Fax sender code (continued)

```
                text,
                textType);

        if (result > 0)
        {

            // Positive returned value indicates that the fax was
            // sent successfully.
            // The return value is the Transaction ID.
            System.out.println(
                "Fax submitted properly. Transaction number: "
                    + result);
            return true;
        } else
        {
            // Negative returned value indicates sending failure.
            // See error code definitions
            System.out.println(
                "Error sending fax!  Error code " + result);
            return false;
        }
    } catch (Exception e)
    {
        e.printStackTrace();
        return false;
    }
}

public String getText()
{
    return text;
}

public void setText(String text)
{
    this.text = text;
}

public String getTextType()
{
    return textType;
}

public void setTextType(String textType)
{
    this.textType = textType;
}

public String getResult()
{
    return Long.toString(result);
}
```

Example 6-4. Fax sender code (continued)

```
    public static void main(String[] args)
    {
        FaxSender test = new FaxSender();
        test.setTextType(TEXT);
        test.setText("This is a test.");
        System.out.println(test.sendFax());
        System.out.println("Done!");
    }
}
```

The code shown in Example 6-4 uses a standard Apache Axis SOAP service. To use this code, generate the bindings using the Apache Axis tools (as originally described in Chapter 3). The command that generates the InterFAX code is shown in Example 6-5.

Example 6-5. Generating the InterFAX bindings

```
C:\devenv\axis-1_1\lib>java –classpath commons-logging.jar;log4j-1.2.8.jar;
wsdl4j.jar;axis.jar;commons-discovery.jar;jaxrpc.jar;saaj.jar org.apache.axis.wsdl.
WSDL2Java http://ws.interfax.net/dfs.asmx?wsdl
```

Arguably, it's harder to generate the HTML to send as the content of the fax than it actually is to make the call into the fax service and send the fax. As shown in Figure 6-7, you can see that the same HTML formatting used for the email is also used for the fax.

```
address_owner : 1
notify_version : 1.5
address_zip :
payment_fee : 0.01
mc_fee : 0.01
address_state :   A
receiver_id : ZE4CQEBXYWLYQ
quantity : 1
address_status : confirmed
payer_email :          @cascadetg.com
txn_id :
verify_sign :
address_street :
incoming_ip :
payment_type : instant
mc_currency : USD
last_name :
payment_date : 20:29:50 Jan 04, 2004 PST
txn_type : web_accept
paypal_address_id :
address_name :
address_country : United States
ebay_address_id :
custom :
mc_gross : 0.01
payment_status : Completed
item_number :
address_city :
payer_id :
receiver_email :         @cascadetg.com
first_name :
tax : 0.00
payer_status : unverified
business :         @cascadetg.com
payment_gross : 0.01
item_name : IPN Test
```

Figure 6-7. Received fax

InterFAX does, of course, charge for faxes sent through their system. The nice thing is that you never need to worry about setting up or maintaining a fax system yourself. While it's possible to envision using the standard Java printing APIs to generate faxes that are sent via a local fax modem, this can rapidly become very complicated and expensive. It certainly takes more time to develop and maintain, plus you'll pay telephone charges.

 If you intend to work with faxes a lot—in particular, if you wish to design nicely formatted faxes—you will likely go mad debugging the results using a normal fax machine. You may wish to consider using a fax-to-email provider such as j2.com (*http://www.j2.com*). There is, of course, a certain pleasant irony in using InterFAX to generate faxes only to then use the j2.com to turn the fax back into an email.

The secure information (such as passwords and account names) has been broken into a separate class. The first, for PayPal, is shown in Example 6-6, and the second, for the InterFAX service, is shown in Example 6-7.

Example 6-6. PayPal tokens

```
package com.cascadetg.ch06;

public class PayPalTokens
{
    // Put your PayPal registered email address here. You want to
    // make sure that payments are sent to the correct address.
    static final String paypalEmail = "test_account@cascadetg.com";

    // Mail configuration
    static final String mailhost = "smtp.mail.myisp.com";
    static final String mailhost_username = "mail_username";
    static final String mailhost_password = "mail_password";
}
```

The code assumes that you must provide authentication to use the target SMTP server (typical for most ISPs today).

Example 6-7. Fax tokens

```
package com.cascadetg.ch06;

public class FaxSenderTokens
{
    public static String faxUsername = "fax_account";
    public static String faxPassword = "fax_password";
    public static String faxDevPartnerID = "12345678;

    public static String faxTestFaxNumber = "0014155551234";
}
```

Notice that the U.S. phone number is shown with a three-digit country code (001) prefixing the 415 (San Francisco area) phone number. Developers in non-U.S. countries are likely used to this method for specifying full phone numbers. If you're not, consult your local phone book for information on country codes and international dialing rules.

You've now used two different web services to provide for an automated sales system and managed to add both fax and email notification capabilities. It's easy to imagine adding even more capabilities as the support organization grows.

CHAPTER 7

Project 4: Syndicated Search

This chapter looks at a generating an RSS[*] (most commonly, Really Simple Syndication) feed using the results obtained from a Google search. In a sense, you can say that this is an example of a web service gateway. RSS offers a translation from a SOAP web service to a syndication feed more accessible via a variety of content management systems and news aggregators.

In brief, RSS is a simple XML format for describing a series of entries, with links back to full stories. Popular uses include providing summaries of news stories and also personal weblog entries, but an increasing number of systems are offering feeds for other purposes, such as a feed containing status information on a remote system. In any event, a variety of software tools—both desktop and web-based—have evolved for watching RSS feeds.

One of the best uses for RSS is monitoring search results from sites such as Google (*http://www.google.com*). Many people take their Google search results very seriously. There are businesses that depend on their Google rankings for customer traffic, or as a metric for their web-site success and popularity. For people that spend a lot of time worrying about this, they may have several search terms they wish to monitor. By providing Google search results as RSS feeds, users can monitor their Google search results using a RSS aggregator.

The sample application built in this chapter shows how to leverage the existing Google APIs to provide RSS feeds. In effect, this application acts as a gateway between two different kinds of application: a SOAP-based service and a syndication-oriented RSS feed. The users of the application don't need to know anything about web services to take advantage of the data published by Google; they simply need to add a URL to their RSS aggregator.

---

[*] RSS is one of those acronyms about which people argue the meaning of the letters, but which everyone refers to simply as "RSS" and pretends that they're all talking about the same thing. The RSS 2.0 specification, posted at *http://blogs.law.harvard.edu/tech/rss*, describes it as Really Simple Syndication, which is what I'll use as a "canonical" RSS definition, although the RSS 0.91 specification enjoys much wider adoption.

Making Feeds Available

Before a user can subscribe to a feed, she needs some mechanism to know the feed is available. The most obvious mechanism for this is posting the feed's URL on a web page. Let's start by looking at the web page that lists the feeds. You can see these three feeds (a XML icon next to the text View RSS is a typical user interface element for indicating an RSS feed) in Figure 7-1.

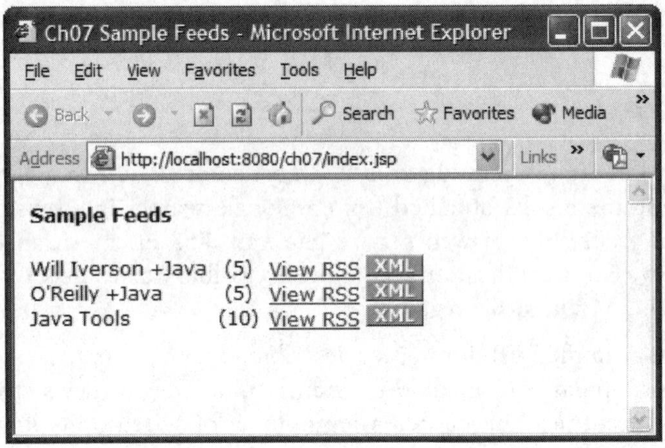

Figure 7-1. Available feeds

Clicking on the link for the O'Reilly +Java feed shows the feed being generated for a Google search for the term, O'Reilly +Java, as shown in Figure 7-2.

Notice that the feed includes HTML tags embedded in the description and titles. The RSS specification is a bit ambiguous about embedded HTML, and it's easy to think of reasons why embedded HTML can be both a good and a bad thing. Unfortunately, there is absolutely no standardization of how HTML in feeds should be treated—which can potentially confuse XML parsers—and parsing HTML by hand is a tedious, error-prone operation. In this particular instance, the feeds are by definition coming from Google, and Google emits fairly consistent data, so the application passes the limited formatting (principally boldfacing certain terms) along to the user.

Let's look at the JSP page that generates these RSS files in Example 7-1.

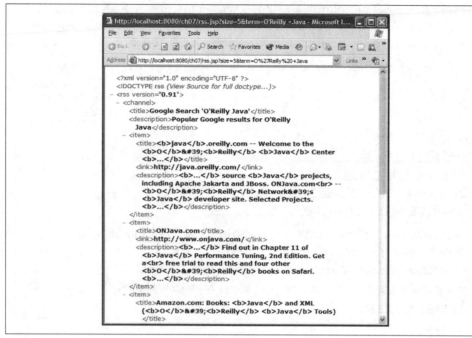

Figure 7-2. O'Reilly +Java RSS feed

Example 7-1. RSS JSP

```
<%@
page contentType="text/xml;charset=utf-8" language="java" %><%@
page import="com.cascadetg.ch07.FeedGenerator"          %><%
response.setContentType("text/xml");

FeedGenerator myFeed = new FeedGenerator( );
String term = request.getParameter("term");
int size = 5;
if(request.getParameter("size") != null)
    size = Integer.parseInt(request.getParameter("size"));

%><%= myFeed.getChannel(term, FeedGenerator.RSS_091, size) %>
```

Examining RSS Feed Generation

As you look over Example 7-1, you can see that a bit of care is taken to avoid producing spurious return characters in the generated text: the %> and <% delimiters are placed directly next to each other. Also notice that the JSP page looks for two parameters: the search term (term) and the number of items (size) to return. After interpreting the incoming parameters, it is passed to a FeedGenerator object (notice that the default is RSS 0.91, not the latest 2.0 specification).

Our Java code relies on a third-party library, called Informa, to both parse and generate RSS files. You can download Informa from *http://informa.sourceforge.net/*. To install, simply place the informa.jar library in the CLASSPATH.

An overview of the FeedGenerator class can be found in Figure 7-3.

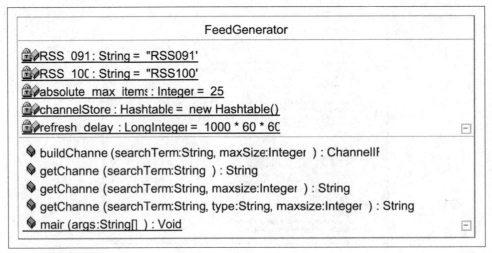

Figure 7-3. FeedGenerator class diagram

The code for the FeedGenerator class in Example 7-2 uses the Google web service code (as initially described in Chapter 4) to retrieve the results and generate a RSS feed using the Informa library. Depending on the needs of the application, one of three FeedGenerator.getChannel( ) methods can be used by client code to retrieve data. A java.util.Hashtable( ) caches data from Google, which ensures that the Google server isn't hit too often.

The default refresh_delay that shows once an hour is too aggressive for production use. You'd be better off using a daily refresh, but once an hour or more often works well for test purposes.

Example 7-2. RSS feed generation

```
package com.cascadetg.ch07;

import java.io.StringWriter;
import java.net.URL;
import java.util.Date;
import java.util.Hashtable;

import de.nava.informa.core.ChannelExporterIF;
import de.nava.informa.core.ChannelIF;
import de.nava.informa.exporters.RSS_1_0_Exporter;
```

Example 7-2. RSS feed generation (continued)

```java
import de.nava.informa.exporters.RSS_0_91_Exporter;
import de.nava.informa.impl.basic.ChannelBuilder;

// We'll be relying on the same straight-forward library as provided
// by Google and described in Chapter 4.
import com.google.soap.search.*;

// We'll be using the same tokens as described in Chapter 4 for
// authorizing the Google search
import com.cascadetg.ch04.DeveloperTokens;

public class FeedGenerator
{
    /**
     * We'll be using this as a repository of already retrived data
     * from Google to avoid hitting the Google server too frequently.
     */
    static Hashtable channelStore = new Hashtable();

    /**
     * This is the refresh delay between checking for new data. Note
     * that this is the most often we will be checking - if a user
     * doesn't request the page after an hour, we aren't going to be
     * out looking for the data.
     */
    static long refresh_delay = 1000 * 60 * 60; // 1 hour

    /** Absolute maximum number of items we'll return to avoid abuse. */
    static int absolute_max_items = 25;

    /**
     * This is the main method for retrieving the data from Google and
     * building it as an Informa RSS object.
     *
     * @param searchTerm
     *              is the String sent to Google as a query
     * @param maxSize
     *              is the maximum number of items to return
     */
    public ChannelIF buildChannel(String searchTerm, int maxSize)
    {

        ChannelIF final_channel = null;

        // First, we need to make sure that the channel requested is
        // not already in the channelStore cache. If it is in the
        // cache, we will check to see how old it is. If it's older
        // than the default refresh, we'll want to get it again
        // anyways.
        if (channelStore.get(searchTerm + "|" + maxSize) != null)
        {
```

Example 7-2. RSS feed generation (continued)

```
        final_channel =
            (ChannelIF)channelStore.get(searchTerm + "|" + maxSize);

        if (final_channel.getLastUpdated( ).getTime( )
            + refresh_delay
            > new Date( ).getTime( ))
        {
            return final_channel;
        }
    }

    try
    {
        ChannelIF channel = null;
        ChannelBuilder myBuilder = new ChannelBuilder( );

        channel =
            myBuilder.createChannel(
                "Google Search '" + searchTerm + "'");
        channel.setDescription(
            "Popular Google results for " + searchTerm);
        channel.setCreator("Google Watcher");

        // Here, we set up the Google search.
        GoogleSearch search = new GoogleSearch( );

        // Set mandatory attributes
        search.setKey(DeveloperTokens.googleKey);
        search.setQueryString(searchTerm);

        // Set optional attributes
        search.setSafeSearch(true);

        // Invoke the actual search. Note that this can be a
        // potentially "expensive" call, as it can easily take 1-3
        // seconds.
        GoogleSearchResult result = search.doSearch( );

        // Here, we take the search results and loop through,
        // adding them as items to the Informa API. Note that we
        // make checks to make sure that we aren't adding too
        // many items.
        if (result != null)
        {
            GoogleSearchResultElement[] mySearchElements =
                result.getResultElements( );

            for (int i = 0; i < mySearchElements.length; i++)
            {
                if (i > absolute_max_items - 1)
                    break;
```

Example 7-2. RSS feed generation (continued)

```
                        if (i > maxSize - 1)
                            break;

                        myBuilder.createItem(
                            channel,
                            mySearchElements[i].getTitle(),
                            mySearchElements[i].getSnippet(),
                            new URL(mySearchElements[i].getURL()));

                    }

                }

                // Finally, we set the timestamp for this channel and add
                // it to the cache.
                channel.setLastUpdated(new Date());
                channelStore.put(searchTerm + "|" + maxSize, channel);

                // Ok, everything looks good, so let's go ahead and return
                // the channel.
                return channel;
            } catch (Exception e)
            {
                e.printStackTrace();
            }

            // If channel is still null, odds are good that there was a
            // failure loading some how. This might be as mundane as a
            // network failure between the JSP server and Google, in which
            // case there's no reason not to return the cached result if
            // available as a backup.
            // Worst case, we still leave channel set to null.
            if (final_channel == null)
            {
                final_channel =
                    (ChannelIF)channelStore.get(searchTerm + "|" + maxSize);
            }

            return final_channel;
    }
```

The code in Example 7-3 shows additional methods, principally designed to ease the integration of the code in Example 7-2 into the application's JSP layer, and also a simple command-line implementation (useful when testing the application).

Example 7-3. RSS feed generation, Part II

```
/**
 * A static constant we use to indicate that an RSS 1.0 feed is
 * requested.
 */
public static final String RSS_100 = "RSS100";
```

Example 7-3. RSS feed generation, Part II (continued)

```java
/**
 * A static constant we use to indicate that an RSS 0.91 feed is
 * requested.
 */
public static final String RSS_091 = "RSS091";

/**
 * A default invocation of a search, with RSS 1.0 and five results
 * returned
 */
public String getChannel(String searchTerm)
{
    return getChannel(searchTerm, RSS_100, 5);
}

/** A default invocation, with RSS 1.0 returned */
public String getChannel(String searchTerm, int maxsize)
{
    return getChannel(searchTerm, RSS_100, maxsize);
}

/**
 * A configurable request for channel as an XML document in the
 * form of a String. If you wished to do additional formatting, you
 * may (for example) want to parse and load this using JDOM or
 * another XML technology.
 *
 * For best performance and ease of use in a JSP application, you'd
 * be better off using the Informa API directly.
 */
public String getChannel(
    String searchTerm,
    String type,
    int maxsize)
{

    // We don't want to write the results to a file on disk - we
    // just want to keep the results in-memory.
    StringWriter myStringWriter = new StringWriter( );

    try
    {
        ChannelExporterIF myExporter = null;

        // Here, we set up a different exporter depending on the
        // requested RSS version.
        if (type.equals(RSS_091))
        {
            myExporter =
                new RSS_0_91_Exporter(myStringWriter, "UTF-8");

        } else
```

Example 7-3. RSS feed generation, Part II (continued)

```
        {
            myExporter =
                new RSS_1_0_Exporter(myStringWriter, "UTF-8");
        }

        // Here, we go off to our earlier method and actually do
        // the 'heavy lifting' to build the channel.
        ChannelIF myChannel = buildChannel(searchTerm, maxsize);

        // Now, just write the results into the StringWriter.
        myExporter.write(myChannel);
    } catch (Exception e)
    {
        e.printStackTrace();
    }
    return myStringWriter.toString();
}

/**
 * A command-line diagnostic, lets you retrieve a set of results
 * and reports some simple timing data.
 */
public static void main(String[] args)
{
    FeedGenerator myFeed = new FeedGenerator();
    long last_time = new Date().getTime();
    long timing = new Date().getTime() - last_time;

    String term = "Mac OS X for Java Geeks";
    System.out.println(myFeed.getChannel(term));
    timing = new Date().getTime() - last_time;
    System.out.print(timing + " ");
    System.out.println(term);

    last_time = new Date().getTime();
    System.out.println(myFeed.getChannel(term));
    timing = new Date().getTime() - last_time;
    System.out.print(timing + " ");
    System.out.println(term);

    last_time = new Date().getTime();
    System.out.println(myFeed.getChannel(term));
    timing = new Date().getTime() - last_time;
    System.out.print(timing + " ");
    System.out.println(term);

    last_time = new Date().getTime();
    term = "Google innovations";
    System.out.println(myFeed.getChannel(term));
    timing = new Date().getTime() - last_time;
    System.out.print(timing + " ");
    System.out.println(term);
```

Example 7-3. RSS feed generation, Part II (continued)

```
        last_time = new Date( ).getTime( );
        System.out.println(myFeed.getChannel(term));
        timing = new Date( ).getTime( ) - last_time;
        System.out.print(timing + " ");
        System.out.println(term);
        last_time = new Date( ).getTime( );
    }
}
```

Using an Aggregator

Now that you've seen how the feed is generated, let's use the feed in a more human-friendly format than raw XML. There are a variety of free, open source, shareware and commercial aggregators of RSS feeds available. Figure 7-4 shows how to add the Google feeds to Awasu Personal, a free aggregator for Windows available from *http://www.awasu.com/*. Awasu retrieves the RSS feeds you subscribed to on a user-defined basis (for example, once an hour, once a day, once a week, etc.).

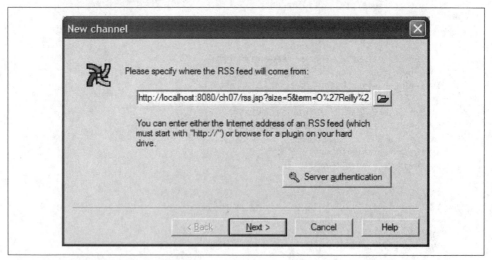

Figure 7-4. Adding a feed to an aggregator

Once the feed has been added, it's visible along with other feeds, as shown in Figure 7-5.

There are a variety of other aggregators that serve different purposes:

Aggie
> *http://bitworking.org/Aggie.html*; Windows only

Aggreg8
> *http://www.aggreg8.net/*; based on Mozilla XUL

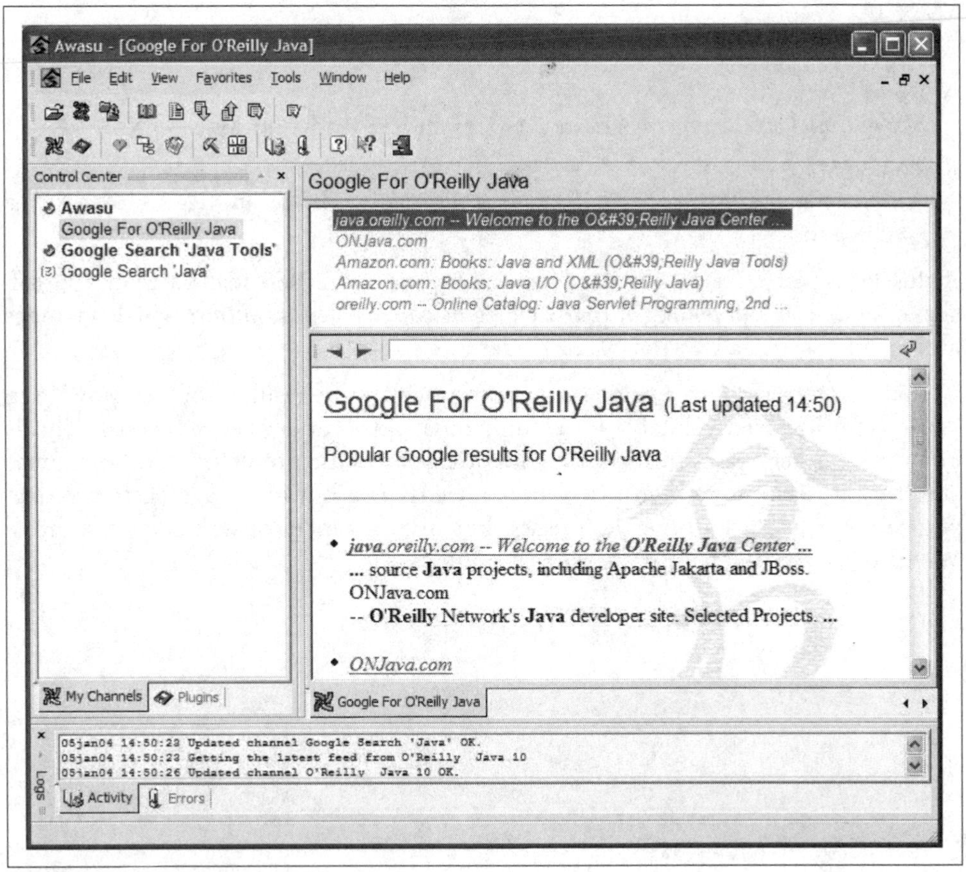

Figure 7-5. Viewing RSS in an aggregator

AmphetaDesk
> *http://www.disobey.com/amphetadesk/*; for Mac OS X, Windows, and Linux

Bloglines
> *http://www.bloglines.com/*; a web site that aggregates for you

FeedDemon
> *http://www.feeddemon.com/*; a commercial, Windows-only reader

Fetch!
> *http://www.enterpriserss.com/*; an "enterprise" RSS package for Windows only

Friday
> *http://members.bellatlantic.net/~vze3szvh/friday/*; a Java-based reader designed for small devices (specifically, devices that support the J2ME standard)

Genecast
> *http://www.genecast.com/*; converts RSS feeds to NNTP (the protocol behind Usenet, a.k.a. "newsgroups")

Meerkat
  http://www.oreillynet.com/meerkat/; O'Reilly's open wire service based on RSS

NetNewsWire
  http://ranchero.com/netnewswire/; a popular RSS reader for Mac OS X

Radio Userland
  http://radio.userland.com/whatIsANewsAggregator; both an aggregator and a weblog tool

If this list doesn't meet your needs, you can find more RSS readers than you can shake a stick at by visiting *http://www.lights.com/weblogs/rss.html*, which includes among other gems, a Newton-based reader.

In this chapter, we built a bridge service to translate the results from a "pure" web service into RSS feeds, suitable for reading on a variety of devices. Obviously, this is potentially a very powerful solution for many types of problems, but sometimes you'll want to do more than just generate feeds. You'll want to aggregate the data yourself, not just from other RSS feeds, but from a variety of web service sources. We'll do just that in the next chapter.

CHAPTER 8

Project 5: News Aggregator

In this chapter, we'll build a news-gathering application using Quartz, an open source Java job scheduler. Quartz, which is available at *http://www.quartzscheduler. org/*, provides sophisticated timing and tracking of web service data retrieval from different sources. Some of these have been covered in other chapters of this book, including Amazon, Google, eBay, and RSS. In effect, you will build a *data aggregator*—a system that pools and caches data from the Internet, presenting it in a coherent whole.

This project leverages the code used in prior chapters to access remote web services—in particular, the web service interfaces to Amazon, Google, and eBay as shown in Chapter 4. Once you have established communication with a web service, you can often leverage that connectivity in new ways, presenting the information to users in different ways or even adding entirely new lines of business.

Getting Started

The initial user interface for the aggregator is shown in Figure 8-1. To add a data source to monitor, the user clicks on the New Watcher link.

As you can see in Figure 8-2, a form appears that allows a user to define a data source that should be watched by the application (hence the term "watcher"). The user can specify what precise data should be retrieved and how frequently it should be updated.

One unfortunate user interface element of this application is the use of the watcher target field to get additional data on the specific information. The interpretation of this field varies depending on the type of watcher being created. In a real application, this should be broken up into one or more additional pages with additional validation of the user entered data.

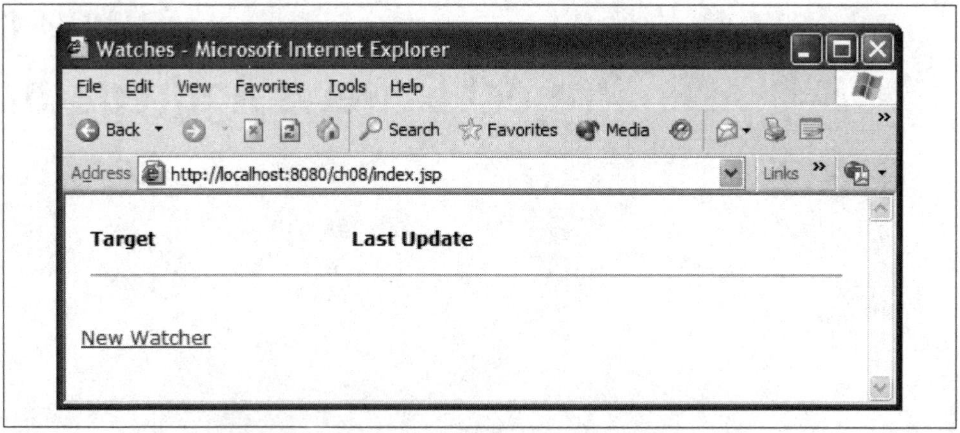

Figure 8-1. Initial interface

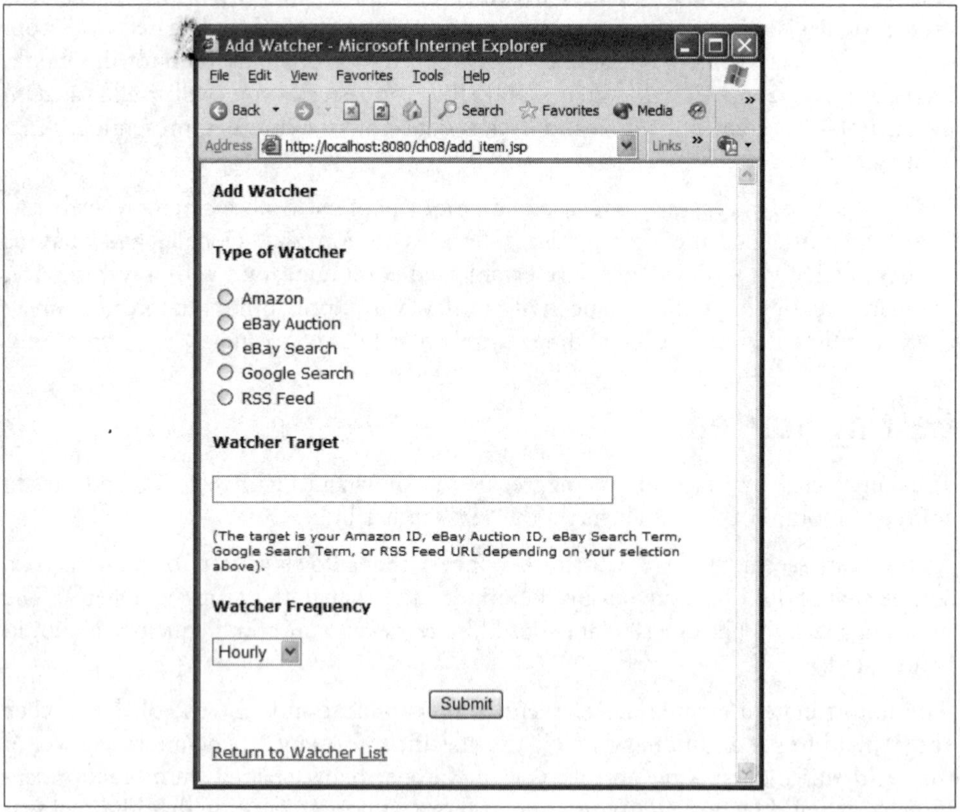

Figure 8-2. Adding a watcher

As shown in Example 8-1, some very minimal validation of the user-entered data is performed. This is done in a single code block at the top of the JSP; the rest of the JSP is primarily concerned with the HTML form.

Example 8-1. Add watcher JSP

```
<%@ page contentType="text/html; charset=iso-8859-1" language="java"
    import="com.cascadetg.ch08.AbstractWatcher"  %>
<%
String error = null;
if(request.getParameter("Submit") != null)
{
    if(request.getParameter("type") == null)
        error = "No Type Defined.";
    if(request.getParameter("target") == null)
    {
        error = "No Target Defined."; }
        else
        {
        if(request.getParameter("target").length() < 1)
        {
            error = "No Target Defined.";
        }
    }
    if(error == null)
    {
        AbstractWatcher.addWatch(request.getParameter("type"),
            request.getParameter("target"),
            request.getParameter("frequency"));
        response.sendRedirect("index.jsp");
        return;
    }

}
if(error == null)
    error = "";
%>
<head>
<title>Add Watcher</title>
<meta http-equiv="Content-Type" content="text/html; charset=iso-8859-1" />
<style type="text/css">
<!--
.smaller {font-size: smaller}
-->
</style>
<link href="../ch04/www/default.css" rel="stylesheet" type="text/css" />
<style type="text/css">
<!--
.warning {color: red}
-->
</style>
</head>
```

Example 8-1. Add watcher JSP (continued)

```
<body>
<form name="form1" id="form1" method="post" action="">
  <p><strong>Add Watcher<hr />
  <span class="warning"><%= error %></span></strong>
  <p><strong>Type of Watcher</strong></p>
  <p>
  <%
  int types = AbstractWatcher.getTypes(false).length;
  for(int i = 0; i < types; i++) { %>
    <input name="type" type="radio" value="<%= AbstractWatcher.getTypes(false)[i] %>" />
    <%= AbstractWatcher.getTypes(true)[i] %><br />
  <% } %>
  <p><strong>Watcher Target</strong></p>
  <p>
    <input name="target" type="text" size="50" />
  </p>
  <p>    <span class="smaller">(The target is your Amazon ID, eBay Auction ID,
eBay Search Term, Google Search Term, or RSS Feed URL depending on your
selection above).</span></p>
  <p><strong>Watcher Frequency</strong></p>
  <p>    <select name="frequency">
      <option value="Hourly" selected="selected">Hourly</option>
      <option value="Daily">Daily</option>
      <option value="Weekly">Weekly</option>
      </select>
  </p>
  <p align="center">
    <input type="submit" name="Submit" value="Submit" />
</p>
  <p align="left"><a href="index.jsp">Return to Watcher List</a> </p>
</form>
</body>
</html>
```

Selecting Amazon and entering an Amazon ID brings us back to the *index.jsp* page,
as shown in Figure 8-3. In addition to the expected information about the selected
product, there's now additional data showing the time of the last update, as well as
an option to delete the watcher.

Deleting a Watcher

Figure 8-4 shows the confirmation form presented when a user clicks the delete link.

The code to present the deletion form is shown in Example 8-2. A small amount of
validation is performed at the top of the page; otherwise, the JSP is mostly concerned with the user interface.

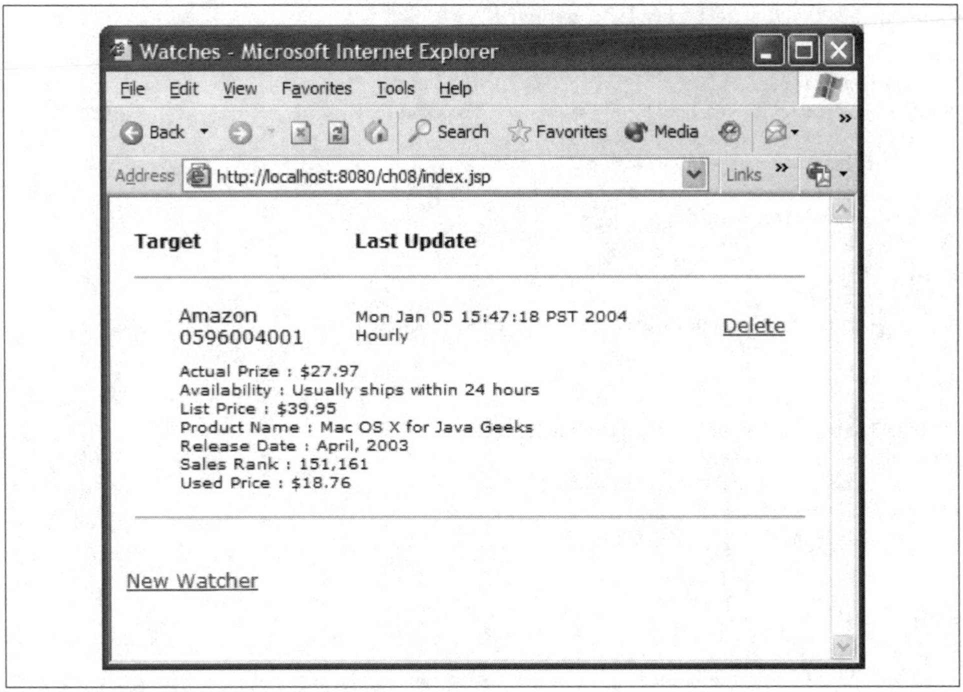

Figure 8-3. Added watcher

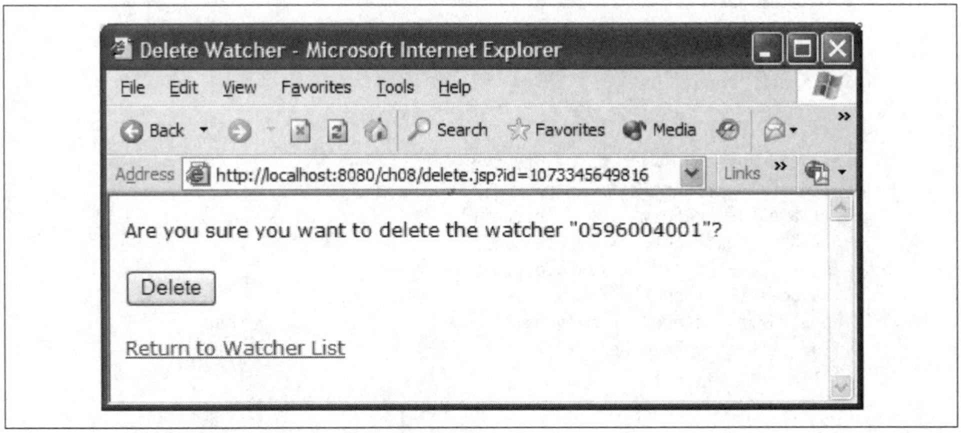

Figure 8-4. Deleting a watcher

Example 8-2. Deleting a watcher JSP

```
<%@ page contentType="text/html; charset=iso-8859-1"
language="java" errorPage="" %>
<!DOCTYPE html PUBLIC "-//W3C//DTD XHTML 1.0 Transitional//EN"
"http://www.w3.org/TR/xhtml1/DTD/xhtml1-transitional.dtd">
<html xmlns="http://www.w3.org/1999/xhtml">
```

Example 8-2. Deleting a watcher JSP (continued)

```jsp
<%
    boolean delete = false;
    String productID = request.getParameter("productID");
    if(request.getParameter("Delete") != null)
        delete = true;

    boolean deleted = false;
    if(delete)
    {
      deleted =
        com.cascadetg.ch04.Search.removeSearch(productID);
    };
%>
<head>
<title>Chapter 4: Competitive Analysis</title>
<meta http-equiv="Content-Type"
    content="text/html; charset=iso-8859-1" />
<link href="default.css"
    rel="stylesheet" type="text/css" />
</head>
<body><%
if (delete)
{
    if(deleted)
    {
%>
        <p>The item has been deleted.</p>
<%    } else {
%>
        <p>Item not found.</p>
<%    }
} else{ %>
        <p>Are you sure you want to delete the
            item "<%= productID %>"?</p>
        <form name="deleteForm" id="deleteForm"
            method="post" action="delete.jsp">
         <input type="hidden" name="productID"
          value="<%= productID %>"/>
         <input name="Delete" type="submit"
          id="Delete" value="Delete" />
        </form>
        <%
}
%>
<p><a href="list.jsp">Return to list.</a></p>
</body>
</html>
```

Current Watcher Listing

The code for the main user interface page, as shown in Example 8-3, is centered around looping over the results from the static method, AbstractWatcher. getSortedWatches( ).

Example 8-3. Main interface JSP

```
<%@ page contentType="text/html; charset=iso-8859-1" language="java" import="com.
cascadetg.ch08.AbstractWatcher" %>
<!DOCTYPE html PUBLIC "-//W3C//DTD XHTML 1.0 Transitional//EN" "http://www.w3.org/TR/
xhtml1/DTD/xhtml1-transitional.dtd">
<html xmlns="http://www.w3.org/1999/xhtml">
<head>
<title>Watches</title>
<meta http-equiv="Content-Type" content="text/html; charset=iso-8859-1" />
<link href="../ch04/www/default.css" rel="stylesheet" type="text/css" />
</head>

<body>
<table width="100%" border="0" cellpadding="3" cellspacing="3">
<tr>
  <td colspan="2"><strong>Target</strong></td>
  <td><strong>Last Update </strong></td>
  <td> </td>
</tr>
<tr><td colspan="4"><hr></td></tr>
<%
AbstractWatcher[] myWatches = AbstractWatcher.getSortedWatches();
if(myWatches != null)
{
if(myWatches.length > 0) {
for(int i = 0; i < myWatches.length; i ++ ) {
%>

<tr>
<td width="20"> </td>
<td> <%= myWatches[i].getHumanType( ) %><br />
    <%= myWatches[i].getTarget( ) %></td>
<td>
<small><%= myWatches[i].getLastUpdate( ).toString( ) %><br><%= myWatches[i].getFrequency( )
%></small></td><td>
<a href="delete.jsp?id=<%= myWatches[i].getID( ) %>">Delete</a>
</td></tr>
<% if(myWatches[i].getAttributes( ).size( ) > 0) { %>
<tr><td width="20"> </td>
<td colspan="2"><small>
<%
java.util.Iterator attributeKeys = myWatches[i].getAttributes( ).keySet( ).iterator( );
while(attributeKeys.hasNext( ))
{
    String name = (String)attributeKeys.next( );
    String key = myWatches[i].getFormattedAttribute(name);
```

Example 8-3. Main interface JSP (continued)

```
%>
<%= name %> : <%=key %><br>
<% } %>
</small>
</td><td> </td></tr><% } %>
<tr><td colspan="6"><hr></td></tr>
<% } } } %>
</table>
<p><a href="add_item.jsp">New Watcher</a> </p>
</body>
</html>
```

As shown in Figure 8-5, even a few defined watchers can start to overwhelm the default presentation. It's easy to envision adding additional user-interface functionality to deal with the data being mined, such as a Swing client or a more sophisticated DHTML design.

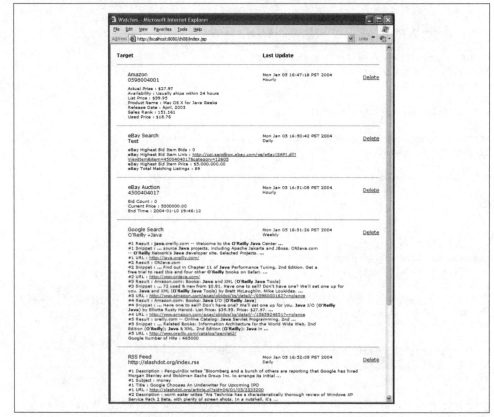

Figure 8-5. Several defined watchers

Watcher Implementation

The code for this application relies on a library called Quartz, a pure Java scheduler. Quartz (*http://www.quartzscheduler.org/*) provides reliable scheduling for tasks. You can define a task schedule with potentially very complex rules (for example, fire a task every weekday at 2 a.m. or once every two hours). The reliability can be achieved using Quartz with a relational database. Quartz can automatically store and update job information in the database via JDBC.

This sample application is less concerned with the broader feature set of Quartz and instead focuses on using Quartz to provide basic job-scheduling capabilities. Therefore, the core of the application is based on an implementation of the interface org.quartz.Job. This interface defines a single method, execute(JobExecutionContext context), called when the task is to be performed. All the data associated with the task is passed in via the org.quartz.JobExecutionContext object.

When the application starts, it initializes a single org.quartz.Scheduler (watcherScheduler) object. Then, as the user adds watchers, the implementation adds an org.quartz.SimpleTrigger and the appropriate org.quartz.Job implementation. That's it: Quartz takes care of calling application tasks, handling the scheduling as needed.

AbstractWatcher Implementation

The underlying Java code for this application is divided into a few basic classes, as shown in Figure 8-6. There's an abstract base, AbstractWatcher, which includes several static access methods for the JSP pages. The rest of the application code consists of concrete implementations of this base class, one for each type of supported Watcher (AmazonWatcher, EBayAuctionWatcher, EBaySearchWatcher, GoogleWatcher, and RSSWatcher). The Job interface is required by Quartz.

 Good design would argue that the static methods for AbstractWatcher should be broken out into another class—for example, a WatcherManager. For our purposes, the scheme shown here is adequate, but this class is clearly on the fine line of needing a refactoring.

The main class, AbstractWatcher, is shown in Example 8-4. The first thing you'll notice about the AbstractWatcher class is that the application relies heavily on the supporting Quartz classes. Our main data store is the Quartz Scheduler object. In addition to the obvious advantage of code reuse, it means that the application relies on the Quartz data storage facilities. In this example, the application uses the default RAM-based storage mechanism, but it's possible to use the built-in Quartz data

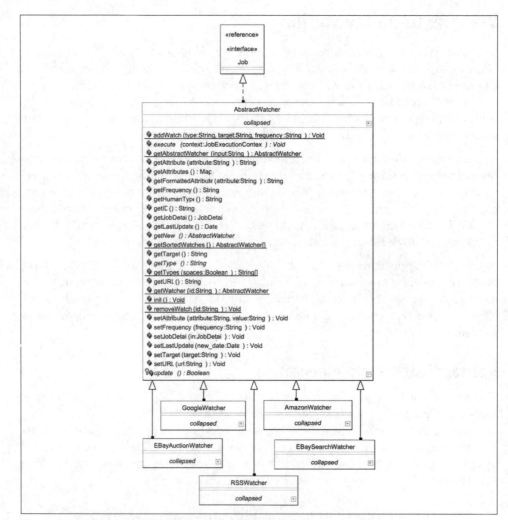

Figure 8-6. Watcher class hierarchy

storage facilities (as described at *http://quartz.sourceforge.net/firstTutorial. html#jobStores*) to save the queue and related data to a supported relational database.

Example 8-4. AbstractWatcher.java

```
package com.cascadetg.ch08;

import java.util.Hashtable;
import org.quartz.*;

public abstract class AbstractWatcher implements Job
{

    static final boolean debug = false;
```

Example 8-4. AbstractWatcher.java (continued)

```java
static Scheduler watcherScheduler = null;

static final Object[] watchers =
    {
        new AmazonWatcher(),
        new EBayAuctionWatcher(),
        new EBaySearchWatcher(),
        new GoogleWatcher(),
        new RSSWatcher()};

/** Constant for use with the frequency. */
static public final String hourly = "Hourly";
/** Constant for use with the frequency. */
static public final String daily = "Daily";
/** Constant for use with the frequency. */
static public final String weekly = "Weekly";

/**
 * This is the main method that is required to be implemented. If
 * the update completes successfully, it should return true,
 * otherwise, return false.
 */
abstract boolean update();

abstract public void execute(JobExecutionContext context)
    throws JobExecutionException;

public abstract AbstractWatcher getNew();

static public void init()

{
    try
    {
        if (watcherScheduler == null)
        {
            SchedulerFactory schedulerFactory =
                new org.quartz.impl.StdSchedulerFactory();
            watcherScheduler = schedulerFactory.getScheduler();
            watcherScheduler.start();
        }

    } catch (Exception e)
    {
        e.printStackTrace();
    }
}

/** The (human-readable) description of the type of Watcher */
public abstract String getType();
```

Example 8-4. AbstractWatcher.java (continued)

```java
public static AbstractWatcher getAbstractWatcher(String input)
{
    for (int i = 0; i < watchers.length; i++)
    {
        if (input.equals(((AbstractWatcher)watchers[i]).getType()))
            return ((AbstractWatcher)watchers[i]).getNew();
    }

    return null;
}

public static String[] getTypes(boolean spaces)
{
    String[] temp =
        {
            new AmazonWatcher().getType(),
            new EBayAuctionWatcher().getType(),
            new EBaySearchWatcher().getType(),
            new GoogleWatcher().getType(),
            new RSSWatcher().getType()};
    if (spaces)
        for (int i = 0; i < temp.length; i++)
            temp[i] = temp[i].replace('_', ' ');

    return temp;
}

public static AbstractWatcher[] getSortedWatches()
{
    init();
    java.util.TreeMap map =
        new java.util.TreeMap(java.text.Collator.getInstance());
    try
    {
        if (watcherScheduler
            .getJobNames(Scheduler.DEFAULT_GROUP)
            .length
            == 0)
            return null;
        String[] keys =
            watcherScheduler.getJobNames(Scheduler.DEFAULT_GROUP);
        for (int i = 0; i < keys.length; i++)
        {
            AbstractWatcher temp = getWatcher(keys[i]);

            map.put(
                temp.getLastUpdate() + " " + temp.getType(),
                temp);
        }
    } catch (SchedulerException e)
```

Example 8-4. AbstractWatcher.java (continued)

```java
    {
        e.printStackTrace( );
    }

    Object[] myCollection = map.values( ).toArray( );
    AbstractWatcher[] result =
        new AbstractWatcher[myCollection.length];
    for (int i = myCollection.length - 1; i >= 0; i--)
        result[i] = (AbstractWatcher)myCollection[i];
    return result;
}

public static AbstractWatcher getWatcher(String id)
{
    try
    {
        JobDetail myJob =
            watcherScheduler.getJobDetail(
                id,
                Scheduler.DEFAULT_GROUP);
        AbstractWatcher temp =
            getAbstractWatcher(
                (String)myJob.getJobDataMap( ).get("type"));
        temp.setJobDetail(myJob);

        return temp;
    } catch (Exception e)
    {
        e.printStackTrace( );
    }
    return null;
}

static final long MINUTE = 60L * 1000L;
static final long HOUR = 60L * 60L * 1000L;
static final long DAY = 24L * 60L * 60L * 1000L;
static final long WEEK = 7L * 24L * 60L * 60L * 1000L;

public static void addWatch(
    String type,
    String target,
    String frequency)
{
    AbstractWatcher myWatcher = getAbstractWatcher(type);
    myWatcher.setTarget(target);
    myWatcher.setFrequency(frequency);
    myWatcher.update( );
    new_id++;
    myWatcher.id = new_id;

    long timing = HOUR;
    if (frequency.equals(daily))
```

Example 8-4. AbstractWatcher.java (continued)

```
            timing = DAY;
        if (frequency.equals(weekly))
            timing = WEEK;

        if (debug)
            timing = MINUTE;

        SimpleTrigger trigger =
            new SimpleTrigger(
                myWatcher.getID( ) + "",
                Scheduler.DEFAULT_GROUP,
                new java.util.Date( ),
                null,
                SimpleTrigger.REPEAT_INDEFINITELY,
                timing);

        init( );
        try
        {
            watcherScheduler.scheduleJob(
                myWatcher.getJobDetail( ),
                trigger);
        } catch (Exception e)
        {
            e.printStackTrace( );

        }
    }

    public static void removeWatch(String id)
    {
        try
        {
            watcherScheduler.deleteJob(id, Scheduler.DEFAULT_GROUP);
        } catch (SchedulerException e)
        {
            e.printStackTrace( );
        }

    }

    private String target = null;
    /** The meaning of the target depends on the type of Watcher. */
    public String getTarget( )
    {
        return target;
    }
    /** The meaning of the target depends on the type of Watcher. */
    public void setTarget(String target)
    {
        this.target = target;
    }
```

Example 8-4. AbstractWatcher.java (continued)

```java
private String frequency = hourly;
/** The frequency the Watcher will be updated. Defaults to hourly. */
public void setFrequency(String frequency)
{
    this.frequency = frequency;
}
/** The frequency the Watcher will be updated */
public String getFrequency()
{
    return frequency;
}

private String url;
public String getURL()
{
    return url;
}
public void setURL(String url)
{
    this.url = url;
}

private java.util.Date last_update = new java.util.Date();
public java.util.Date getLastUpdate()
{
    return last_update;
}
public void setLastUpdate(java.util.Date new_date)
{
    last_update = new_date;
}

Hashtable attributes = new Hashtable();
public java.util.Map getAttributes()
{
    java.util.TreeMap map =
        new java.util.TreeMap(java.text.Collator.getInstance());
    map.putAll(attributes);

    return map;
}
public void setAttribute(String attribute, String value)
{
    if (attribute == null)
        return;
    if (value == null)
        return;
    attributes.put(attribute, value);
}
public String getAttribute(String attribute)
{
    return (String)attributes.get(attribute);
```

Example 8-4. AbstractWatcher.java (continued)

```java
    }
    public String getFormattedAttribute(String attribute)
    {
        String temp = (String)attributes.get(attribute);
        if (temp.startsWith("http://"))
        {
            StringBuffer wrapped = new StringBuffer( );
            wrapped.append("<a target='_blank' href='");
            wrapped.append(temp);
            wrapped.append("'>");
            wrapped.append(temp);
            wrapped.append("</a>");
            return wrapped.toString( );
        }
        return temp;
    }

    public String getHumanType( )
    {
        return getType( ).replace('_', ' ');
    }

    static long new_id = System.currentTimeMillis( );
    long id;
    public String getID( )
    {
        return id + "";
    }

    JobDetail jobDetail;
    public JobDetail getJobDetail( )
    {
        if (jobDetail != null)
        {
            return jobDetail;
        }

        jobDetail =
            new JobDetail(
                this.id + "",
                Scheduler.DEFAULT_GROUP,
                this.getClass( ));

        jobDetail.getJobDataMap( ).put("url", url);
        jobDetail.getJobDataMap( ).put("target", target);
        jobDetail.getJobDataMap( ).put("type", this.getType( ));
        jobDetail.getJobDataMap( ).put("frequency", this.getFrequency( ));
        jobDetail.getJobDataMap( ).put("attributes", attributes);
        jobDetail.getJobDataMap( ).put("id", id);
        jobDetail.getJobDataMap( ).put("date", this.getLastUpdate( ));
```

Example 8-4. AbstractWatcher.java (continued)

```
        return jobDetail;
    }

    public void setJobDetail(JobDetail in)
    {
        this.setURL((String)in.getJobDataMap( ).get("url"));
        this.setTarget((String)in.getJobDataMap( ).get("target"));
        this.setFrequency((String)in.getJobDataMap( ).get("frequency"));
        this.attributes =
            (Hashtable)in.getJobDataMap( ).get("attributes");
        this.id = ((Long)in.getJobDataMap( ).get("id")).longValue( );
        this.last_update =
            ((java.util.Date)in.getJobDataMap( ).get("date"));
    }

}
```

The code for adding new watchers contains a constant not used in the application directly, however, the Minute constant, which is used for time intervals, is also useful for debugging purposes. When using the MINUTE constant on a development system, be careful. Most large-scale web service providers (including Google, Amazon, and eBay) block connections considered abusive.

Quartz keeps track of tasks using serialized data. Each instance of a task being run is called a Job. Therefore, the AbstractWatcher class implements the Quartz Job interface and handles the various bookkeeping details that arise when a Job is created, run, and destroyed. For example, the getJobDetail( ) and setJobDetail( ) methods pass data between the AbstractWatcher classes and the associated Quartz JobDetail object.

Quartz creates and deletes instances of the various AbstractWatcher objects as tasks are run. For example, when an Amazon watcher task is added to the list of tasks to be performed, the data relating to the task is stored as a JobDetail object. Later, when the task is executed, the data needed for the task is returned as a JobDetail object. Quartz can be configured to save the data associated with a JobDetail object different ways, including in memory or in a relational database. It's possible to pass in a serialized instance of a Java object, but serialization is notably finicky about versioning. As it is, the sample application shown here relies on simply serializing a java.util.Hashtable object. This allows a developer to rework the underlying implementations without having to worry about the proper versioning of data in the Quartz persistent store. Regardless of how the task implementations are reworked, the stored data is simply an ordinary java.util.Hashtable.

Amazon Watcher

The code for the first watcher, the AmazonWatcher class, is shown in Example 8-5. It relies on the same SOAP access code as originally described in Chapter 4.

Example 8-5. Amazon watcher implementation

```java
package com.cascadetg.ch08;

import org.quartz.JobExecutionContext;
import org.quartz.JobExecutionException;
import com.amazon.soap.*;
import com.cascadetg.ch04.DeveloperTokens;

public class AmazonWatcher extends AbstractWatcher
{

    public String getType( )
    {
        return "Amazon";
    }

    public boolean update( )
    {
        this.setLastUpdate(new java.util.Date( ));

        // Mac OS X for Java Geeks ISBN
        //String isbn = "0596004001";

        try
        {
            AmazonSearchService myAmazonSearchService =
                new AmazonSearchServiceLocator( );
            AmazonSearchPort myAmazonSearchPort =
                myAmazonSearchService.getAmazonSearchPort( );

            AsinRequest myAsinRequest = new AsinRequest( );

            // Use this to set your Amazon Associates ID
            // For more info on Amazon Associates, see...
            // http://www.amazon.com/associates
            myAsinRequest.setTag(DeveloperTokens.amazon_associates);
            myAsinRequest.setDevtag(DeveloperTokens.amazon_token);
            myAsinRequest.setAsin(this.getTarget( ));
            myAsinRequest.setLocale("us");
            myAsinRequest.setType("heavy");

            ProductInfo myProductInfo =
                myAmazonSearchPort.asinSearchRequest(myAsinRequest);

            Details[] myDetailsArray = myProductInfo.getDetails( );
            Details myDetail = null;
            if (myDetailsArray != null)
```

Example 8-5. Amazon watcher implementation (continued)

```
        {
            myDetail = myDetailsArray[0];

            this.setAttribute(
                "Product Name",
                myDetail.getProductName( ));

            this.setAttribute(
                "Release Date",
                myDetail.getReleaseDate( ));

            this.setAttribute(
                "Actual Prize",
                myDetail.getOurPrice( ));

            this.setAttribute(
                "List Price",
                myDetail.getListPrice( ));

            this.setAttribute(
                "Used Price",
                myDetail.getUsedPrice( ));

            this.setAttribute(
                "Sales Rank",
                myDetail.getSalesRank( ));

            this.setAttribute(
                "Availability",
                myDetail.getAvailability( ));

            this.setURL(myDetail.getUrl( ));

        }
    } catch (Exception e)
    {
        e.printStackTrace( );

    }

    return false;
}

public AbstractWatcher getNew( )
{
    return new AmazonWatcher( );
}

public void execute(JobExecutionContext context)
    throws JobExecutionException
{
    context.getJobDetail( ).getJobDataMap( ).put(
```

Example 8-5. Amazon watcher implementation (continued)

```
        "date",
        new java.util.Date( ));
this.setJobDetail(context.getJobDetail( ));
this.update( );
context.getJobDetail( ).setJobDataMap(
    this.getJobDetail( ).getJobDataMap( ));

System.out.println(
    this.getLastUpdate( ).toString( )
        + " - Running Amazon "
        + this.getID( ));

    }
}
```

eBay Auction Watcher

The watcher, shown in Example 8-6, allows a user to monitor a specific auction. The code relies on the eBay access code developed in Chapter 4, in this case, passing in a new eBay verb, GetItem. Setting this to be updated hourly is typical: it's always good to be on top of the auction for a signed collector's edition of Wil Wheaton's *Just a Geek.*

Example 8-6. Monitoring a specific eBay auction

```
package com.cascadetg.ch08;

import org.quartz.*;
import com.cascadetg.ch04.EbayAPISimpleCall;

public class EBayAuctionWatcher extends AbstractWatcher
{

    public String getType( )
    {
        return "eBay_Auction";
    }

    public boolean update( )
    {
        this.setLastUpdate(new java.util.Date( ));

        EbayAPISimpleCall myCall = new EbayAPISimpleCall( );
        myCall.setApiVerb("GetItem");
        myCall.setArgument("Id", this.getTarget( ));
        myCall.setArgument("DetailLevel", 8 + "");
        org.jdom.Document myResults = myCall.executeCall( );

        org.jdom.Element root = myResults.getRootElement( );
        org.jdom.Element item = root.getChild("Item");
```

Example 8-6. Monitoring a specific eBay auction (continued)

```
try
{
    this.setAttribute(
        "Bid Count",
        item.getChildText("BidCount"));
} catch (Exception e)
{
}
try
{
    this.setAttribute(
        "Current Price",
        item.getChildText("CurrentPrice"));
} catch (Exception e)
{
}
try
{
    this.setAttribute("End Time", item.getChildText("EndTime"));
} catch (Exception e)
{
}
try
{
    this.setAttribute(
        "Winning Bidder",
        item.getChild("HighBidder").getChild(
            "User").getChildText(
            "UserId"));
} catch (Exception e)
{
}
try
{
    this.setAttribute(
        "Winning Bidder Email",
        item.getChild("HighBidder").getChild(
            "User").getChildText(
            "Email"));
} catch (Exception e)
{
    System.out.println("No UserID Email Found");
}
try
{
    this.setAttribute(
        "Winning Bidder Feedback",
        item
            .getChild("HighBidder")
            .getChild("User")
            .getChild("Feedback")
            .getChildText("Score"));
```

Example 8-6. Monitoring a specific eBay auction (continued)

```java
    } catch (Exception e)
    {
    }

    return false;
}

public AbstractWatcher getNew( )
{
    return new EBayAuctionWatcher( );
}

/*
 * (non-Javadoc)
 *
 * @see com.cascadetg.ch08.AbstractWatcher#execute(org.quartz.JobExecutionContext)
 */
public void execute(JobExecutionContext context)
    throws JobExecutionException
{
    context.getJobDetail( ).getJobDataMap( ).put(
        "date",
        new java.util.Date( ));
    this.setJobDetail(context.getJobDetail( ));
    this.update( );
    context.getJobDetail( ).setJobDataMap(
        this.getJobDetail( ).getJobDataMap( ));

    System.out.println(
        this.getLastUpdate( ).toString( )
            + " Running eBay Auction "
            + this.getID( ));

    }

}
```

eBay Search Watcher

The code in Example 8-7 shows how to monitor a particular search query on eBay
(for example, all auctions containing the term "expresso"). The eBay access code in
Chapter 4 actually makes the connection.

Example 8-7. eBay search watcher

```java
package com.cascadetg.ch08;

import org.quartz.JobExecutionContext;
import org.quartz.JobExecutionException;
import com.cascadetg.ch04.EbayAPISimpleCall;
```

Example 8-7. eBay search watcher (continued)

```java
public class EBaySearchWatcher extends AbstractWatcher
{

    public String getType( )
    {
        return "eBay_Search";
    }

    public boolean update( )
    {
        this.setLastUpdate(new java.util.Date( ));

        EbayAPISimpleCall myCall = new EbayAPISimpleCall( );
        myCall.setApiVerb(EbayAPISimpleCall.GetSearchResults);
        myCall.setArgument("Query", this.getTarget( ));
        myCall.setArgument("Order", "MetaHighestPriceSort");
        org.jdom.Document myResults = myCall.executeCall( );

        org.jdom.Element root = myResults.getRootElement( );
        long count =
            Long.parseLong(
                root
                    .getChild("Search")
                    .getChild("GrandTotal")
                    .getText( ));
        this.setAttribute(
            "eBay Total Matching Listings",
            Long.toString(count));

        if (count > 0)
        {
            org.jdom.Element item =
                root.getChild("Search").getChild("Items").getChild(
                    "Item");

            this.setAttribute(
                "eBay Highest Bid Item Price",
                item.getChildText("LocalizedCurrentPrice"));

            this.setAttribute(
                "eBay Highest Bid Item Bids",
                item.getChildText("BidCount"));

            this.setAttribute(
                "eBay Highest Bid Item Link",
                item.getChildText("Link"));
        }
        return false;
    }

    public AbstractWatcher getNew( )
    {
```

Example 8-7. eBay search watcher (continued)

```
        return new EBaySearchWatcher( );
    }

    public void execute(JobExecutionContext context)
        throws JobExecutionException
    {
        context.getJobDetail( ).getJobDataMap( ).put(
            "date",
            new java.util.Date( ));

        this.setJobDetail(context.getJobDetail( ));
        this.update( );
        context.getJobDetail( ).setJobDataMap(
            this.getJobDetail( ).getJobDataMap( ));

        System.out.println(this.getLastUpdate( ).toString( ) +
            " Running eBay Search "
                + this.getID( )
                );

    }
}
```

Google Watcher

The code in Example 8-8 shows a watcher intended to monitor a particular Google search term, relying on the Google SOAP access as defined in Chapter 4. This application is interested in a smaller data set than that shown in Chapters 4 and 7.

Example 8-8. Google watcher

```
package com.cascadetg.ch08;

import org.quartz.JobExecutionContext;
import org.quartz.JobExecutionException;
import com.google.soap.search.*;
import com.cascadetg.ch04.DeveloperTokens;

public class GoogleWatcher extends AbstractWatcher
{

    public String getType( )
    {
        return "Google_Search";
    }

    public boolean update( )
    {
        this.setLastUpdate(new java.util.Date( ));
```

Example 8-8. Google watcher (continued)

```
        GoogleSearch search = new GoogleSearch( );

        // Set mandatory attributes
        search.setKey(DeveloperTokens.googleKey);
        search.setQueryString(this.getTarget( ));

        // Set optional attributes
        search.setSafeSearch(true);
        // Invoke the actual search
        GoogleSearchResult result = null;
        try
        {
            result = search.doSearch( );
        } catch (GoogleSearchFault e)
        {
            e.printStackTrace( );
        }
        // process the result

        if (result != null)
        {
            this.setAttribute(
                "Google Number of Hits",
                Integer.toString(
                    result.getEstimatedTotalResultsCount( )));

            GoogleSearchResultElement[] mySearchElements =
                result.getResultElements( );

            for (int i = 0; i < mySearchElements.length; i++)
            {
                this.setAttribute(
                    "#" + (i + 1) + " Result ",
                    mySearchElements[i].getTitle( ));

                this.setAttribute(
                    "#" + (i + 1) + " Snippet ",
                    mySearchElements[i].getSnippet( ));

                this.setAttribute(
                    "#" + (i + 1) + " URL ",
                    mySearchElements[i].getURL( ));

                if (i > 3)
                {
                    i = mySearchElements.length + 1;
                }
            }
        }
        return false;
    }
```

Example 8-8. Google watcher (continued)

```
    public AbstractWatcher getNew( )
    {
        return new GoogleWatcher( );
    }

    public void execute(JobExecutionContext context)
        throws JobExecutionException
    {
        context.getJobDetail( ).getJobDataMap( ).put(
            "date",
            new java.util.Date( ));

        this.setJobDetail(context.getJobDetail( ));
        this.update( );
        context.getJobDetail( ).setJobDataMap(
            this.getJobDetail( ).getJobDataMap( ));

        System.out.println(
            this.getLastUpdate( ).toString( )
                + " Running Google "
                + this.getID( ));

    }
}
```

RSS Watcher

Finally, the code in Example 8-9 shows the code for reading an RSS feed. It relies on the Informa library (*http://informa.sourceforge.net/*, originally used in Chapter 7) for parsing the RSS.

Example 8-9. RSS watcher

```
package com.cascadetg.ch08;

import org.quartz.JobExecutionContext;
import org.quartz.JobExecutionException;

import de.nava.informa.core.ChannelIF;
import de.nava.informa.core.ItemIF;
import de.nava.informa.impl.basic.ChannelBuilder;
import de.nava.informa.parsers.RSSParser;

public class RSSWatcher extends AbstractWatcher
{

    public String getType( )
    {
        return "RSS_Feed";
    }
```

Example 8-9. RSS watcher (continued)

```java
public boolean update( )
{
    this.setLastUpdate(new java.util.Date( ));

    try
    {
        java.net.URL inpFile = new java.net.URL(this.getTarget( ));
        ChannelIF channel =
            RSSParser.parse(new ChannelBuilder( ), inpFile);

        this.setAttribute(
            "Site Description",
            channel.getDescription( ));
        this.setAttribute("Site URL", channel.getSite( ).toString( ));

        Object[] items = channel.getItems( ).toArray( );
        for (int i = 0; i < items.length; i++)
        {
            ItemIF current = (ItemIF)items[i];
            try
            {
                if (current.getTitle( ).length( ) > 0)
                    if (!current.getTitle( ).equals("<No Title>"))
                        this.setAttribute(
                            "#" + (i + 1) + " Title",
                            current.getTitle( ));
            } catch (Exception e)
            {
            }
            try
            {
                if (current.getLink( ) != null)
                    this.setAttribute(
                        "#" + (i + 1) + " URL",
                        current.getLink( ).toString( ));
            } catch (Exception e)
            {
            }
            try
            {
                if (current.getSubject( ).length( ) > 0)
                    this.setAttribute(
                        "#" + (i + 1) + " Subject",
                        current.getSubject( ));
            } catch (Exception e)
            {
            }
            try
            {
                String temp = current.getDescription( );
                if (temp.length( ) > 255)
                {
```

Example 8-9. RSS watcher (continued)

```
                    temp = temp.substring(0, 253);
                    temp = temp + "...";
                }
                temp = replaceToken(temp, "<", "&lt;");
                temp = replaceToken(temp, ">", "&gt;");
                if (temp.length() > 0)
                    this.setAttribute(
                        "#" + (i + 1) + " Description",
                        temp);

            } catch (Exception e)
            {
            }
            if (i > 3)
            {
                i = items.length + 1;
            }
        }

    } catch (Exception e)
    {
        e.printStackTrace();
    }
    return false;
}

public AbstractWatcher getNew()
{
    return new RSSWatcher();
}

public void execute(JobExecutionContext context)
    throws JobExecutionException
{
    context.getJobDetail().getJobDataMap().put(
        "date",
        new java.util.Date());

    this.setJobDetail(context.getJobDetail());
    this.update();
    context.getJobDetail().setJobDataMap(
        this.getJobDetail().getJobDataMap());
    System.out.println(
        this.getLastUpdate().toString()
            + " Running RSS "
            + this.getID());

}

/** All parameters must not be null. */
static public String replaceToken(
    String input,
```

Example 8-9. RSS watcher (continued)

```
                  String token,
                  String value)
    {
         if (input == null)
              throw new NullPointerException("replaceToken input is null");
         if (token == null)
              throw new NullPointerException("replaceToken token is null");
         if (value == null)
              throw new NullPointerException("replaceToken value is null");

         boolean done = false;
         int current = 0;
         int last = 0;
         StringBuffer results = new StringBuffer("");
         while (!done)
         {
              last = current;
              current = input.indexOf(token, current);
              if (current == -1)
                   done = true;
              if (!done)
              {
                   results.append(input.substring(last, current));
                   results.append(value);
                   current = current + token.length();
              } else
              {
                   results.append(input.substring(last));
              }
         }

         if (input.length() > 0)
              if (results.toString().length() == 0)
                   return input;

         return results.toString();
    }
}
```

The code shown in Example 8-9 is, interestingly, the longest of the watchers (despite relying on the Informa library) and also the most awkward. The reason for this is a basic problem with RSS: too much of the flow of RSS isn't properly defined (or at least, wildly and creatively interpreted).

Informa includes support for aggregation of RSS feeds, as well as relational database persistence, independent of the support provided by Quartz. If you are building an RSS reader application only, you may just want to use the support built into Informa instead. Regardless, it doesn't solve the inherent problems with RSS.

Some RSS feeds literally return the entire text of their article as their description, complete with formatting. A few feeds with a few complete articles in each feed can completely overwhelm the formatting of the page. You can't just chop the feed description at a certain point without dealing with the possibility of embedded HTML as well; an opening < character with no closing tag will ruin your page. Here I replace the < and > characters with the equivalent HTML entities, which means that end users will see the tags interspersed in the text and chop the text after a certain point. It might be better to simply strip the contents of the tags, but at times, certain entries will consist of nothing but (for example) an IMG tag pointing to an interesting graphic. Stripping tags in that instance means that the feed entry will appear to be empty. You might look for IMG tags and replace them with text such as [Image here], perhaps looking for the alt text. Soon, however, the logic for this starts to approach a minimal web browser, and your code is much more complex.

Going Further with Quartz

The sophistication of the Quartz scheduler allows you to provide for much richer job scheduling than that shown. You can build custom Quartz Calendar objects to describe arbitrary schedules (for example, a custom Quartz Calendar object might be provided to indicate company holidays). The infrastructure shown here shows how this scheduling system can be combined with other libraries and various web services to provide a new, rich form of data manipulation beyond that which can be provided by (for example) scraping HTML.

Beyond web services, Quartz allows you to add the notion of "time" to your application in a very durable fashion. For example, let's say that you wish to send an email reminding users to register a downloaded product exactly twice, once after a day and once after a week. Leveraging Quartz allows you to reliably build this sort of functionality into your application (date and time calculations in particular can be difficult, especially if the application goes offline for a period of time). For a broader discussion of Quartz and a detailed comparison with the basic functionality provided by java.util.Timer, see "Job Scheduling in Java," by Dejan Bosanac (*http://www.onjava.com/pub/a/onjava/2004/03/10/quartz.html*).

One thing that's nice about all of this is the ability to provide a system based on standards (in particular, XML and the various web services). The next chapter looks at a system which relies on a somewhat more archaic format.

CHAPTER 9

Project 6: Audio CD Catalog

Although in this day and age of MP3, AAC, and OGG the audio CD feels a bit retro, it's still one of the most popular media formats of all time. As any audio purveyor will tell you, a solid collection of audio CDs can represent considerable investment in time, energy, and emotion.

In this chapter, you will use two web service providers to build an online catalog of audio CDs (and as a by-product, calculate the list value of the collection).

CDDB

Audio CDs, surprisingly, contain no information about the music on the CD. A medium that affords over 600 MB of disk space, oddly, can't find the room to store even a small bit of text describing the artist, the names of the tracks, copyright information—nothing. A few modern CDs are specially crafted to make them hard to rip or contain extra bonus media, but you won't find anything about the audio contents.

To resolve this problem, most popular audio CD conversion applications calculate a fingerprint for the audio CD, connecting via the Internet to retrieve the audio CD artist, album, and track listing information from a server. The server maintains a set of fingerprints and information in a database. Unfortunately, computing the audio CD fingerprint requires lower-level access to the CD drive than is afforded by Java, so a native extension is required to compute the fingerprint.

The original system for storing audio CD track and listing information was simply called CDDB, short for CD database. Eventually, the servers and system were organized as a commercial entity, which renamed itself Gracenote (*http://www.gracenote.com/*). Gracenote renamed the original protocol CDDB1 and deprecated it in favor of a new, proprietary protocol, CDDB2. Commercial developers who wish to use the Gracenote CDDB system are required to purchase a license from Gracenote.

An open source project, freedb (*http://www.freedb.org/*), based on the original CDDB1 protocol, offers similar services to those offered by Gracenote without a fee.

Here, because it's the most accessible and flexible format, you'll create an application that uses the freedb.org database and the CDDB1 protocol to retrieve data. The CDDB1 protocol, as described at:

http://www.freedb.org/modules.php?name= Sections&sop=viewarticle&artid=28

is a throwback to classic Internet protocols. It's based on exchanging very specialized, specific text commands back and forth. Instead of XML, it's based on exchanging text strings and integer error codes.

Fortunately, our application is rescued from the gory details of the handling of the CDDB1 protocol, because it uses an existing (GPL) library provided by Holger Antelmann at *http://www.antelmann.com/developer/*. You'll want to download both the *antelmann.jar* file and the supporting *CDDriveWin.dll* file from:

http://www.antelmann.com/developer/downloads.htm

The *antelmann.jar* file should be placed in your class path, and the *CDDriveWin.dll* must go in the system search path for loading DLLs (e.g., on Windows XP, a reasonable place is your *C:\WINDOWS* directory).

 If you are interested in supporting additional, non-Windows operating systems, the source uses a simple JNI hook for the library. You will need to consult the documentation for your operating system and also build a native JNI library binding to the CD drive interface. For more information, see:

- *http://www.antelmann.com/developer/javadoc/com/antelmann/ cddb/CDDriveSample.html*
- *http://www.antelmann.com/developer/javadoc/com/antelmann/ cddb/CDDrive.html*

Building a CD Catalog

As shown in Figure 9-1, you can see the results of running the application and adding a few CDs.

To add a new CD, simply insert a CD into the drive, and click the Add CD button. The application then reads the inserted CD, uses the native library to calculate the fingerprint for the CD, retrieves the information on the CD from freedb.org, and uses that information to load the image and pricing information from Amazon. It's easy to imagine a DJ loading in favorite CDs and posting a list of recommended disks, complete with links back to Amazon.

The JSP code for the interface, as shown in Example 9-1, is mainly concerned with retrieving the CD data from our Java code and formatting it in HTML. The small bit of logic at the top of the listing checks to see if the form submission button has been

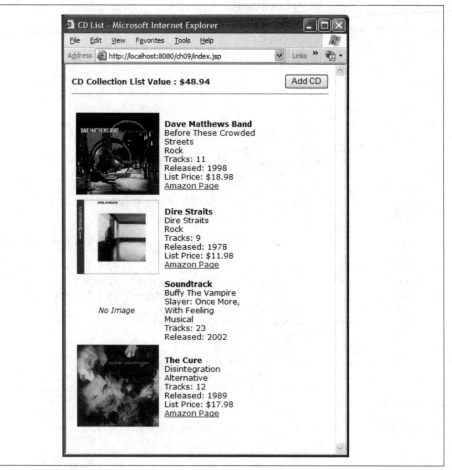

Figure 9-1. Sample CD catalog

clicked by the user. If so, it calls a static method of a Java class to begin processing the newly inserted audio CD.

Example 9-1. CD collection JSP

```
<%@ page contentType="text/html; charset=iso-8859-1"
language="java" import="com.cascadetg.ch09.*" %>
<%
if(request.getParameter("Submit") != null)
{
    CDManager.addCD( );
}
%>
<html xmlns="http://www.w3.org/1999/xhtml">
<head>
<title>CD List</title>
```

Example 9-1. CD collection JSP (continued)

```
<meta http-equiv="Content-Type"
content="text/html; charset=iso-8859-1" />
<link href="../ch04/www/default.css" rel="stylesheet"
type="text/css" />
</head>
<body>
   <% Object[] cds;
cds = CDManager.getCDs().values().toArray();
%><form name="form1" id="form1" method="post" action="">
   <table width="100%" border="0" cellpadding="0" cellspacing="0">
     <tr valign="center"><td><strong>CD Collection List Value :
$<%= CDManager.getListValue() %></strong></td>
     <td align="right" valign="center">
<input type="submit" name="Submit" value="Add CD" /></td></tr>
<tr><td colspan="2"><hr /></td></tr></table></form>

    <% for(int i = 0; i < cds.length; i++) { CD current = (CD)cds[i];%><table width="300">
     <tr>
     <td align="center" width="140"><%
if(current.amazonDetails != null) { %><img src="<%= current.amazonDetails.
getImageUrlMedium()%>"> <% } else        { %><I>No Image</I><% } %></td>
     <% if(current.cddbDetails != null) { %>
     <td><b><%= current.cddbDetails.readArtist()%></b><br>
     <%= current.cddbDetails.readCDTitle()%><br>
     <%= current.cddbDetails.readGenre()%><br>
     Tracks: <%= current.cddbDetails.readNumberOfTracks()%><br>
     Released: <%= current.cddbDetails.readYear()%><br><% } %>
     <% if(current.amazonDetails != null) { %>List Price: <%= current.amazonDetails.
getListPrice()%><br>
     <a href="<%=
current.getAmazonLink()%>" target="_blank">Amazon Page</a></td><%
} %>
     </tr>
</table><% } %>
</body>
</html>
```

The supporting Java class, shown in Example 9-2, serves as a data holder for the information returned from the Amazon web service (in particular, the image information) and the CDDB information. The Details object holds data returned by the Amazon web service. CDID is a com.antelmann class that holds the unique fingerprint of the CD, and the CDDBXmcdParser object holds the record data returned by the CDDB request. Finally, there's a utility method provided that creates a link back to Amazon based on the product ID returned by the Amazon web service.

Example 9-2. Audio CD information

```
package com.cascadetg.ch09;

import com.amazon.soap.Details;
import com.antelmann.cddb.CDDBXmcdParser;
```

Example 9-2. Audio CD information (continued)

```java
import com.antelmann.cddb.CDID;
import com.cascadetg.ch04.DeveloperTokens;

public class CD
{
    public Details amazonDetails;
    public CDDBXmcdParser cddbDetails;
    public CDID cdID;

    public String getAmazonLink( )
    {
        return "http://www.amazon.com/exec/obidos/ASIN/"
            + amazonDetails.getAsin( )
            + "/"
            + DeveloperTokens.amazon_associates
            + "?creative=125581&camp=2321&link_code=as1";
    }
}
```

The real heart of the application can be found in Example 9-3. The JSP from Example 9-1 only used two static methods, both of which are fairly self-descriptive—addCD( ) and getCDs( ). Both are detailed in this class listing. The addCD( ) method kicks off a request to CDDB using the com.antelmann classes. After the results come back, an attempt is made to use the resulting information to look up the results from Amazon based on the artist and CD title.

 The Amazon web service is invoked using the same classes originally developed in Chapter 4.

Example 9-3. Retrieving audio CD information

```java
package com.cascadetg.ch09;

import com.amazon.soap.*;
import com.cascadetg.ch04.*;

import java.util.Enumeration;
import java.util.Hashtable;

public class CDManager
{

    /** Connect to the FreeCDDB using the Antelmann library. */
    public static void addCDDBInfo(CD newCD)
    {

        /*
         * Running in the Tomcat contain confuses the library about
         * where to load the properties configuration file. Therefore,
```

Example 9-3. Retrieving audio CD information (continued)

```
 * we'll just create a set of properties and feed them into the
 * library here.
 */
java.util.Properties newProperties = new java.util.Properties( );
newProperties.setProperty(
    "application.vendor.email",
    "info@antelmann.com");
newProperties.setProperty(
    "application.startCommand",
    "cmd.exe /c start %1");
newProperties.setProperty(
    "user.dir.media",
    "c\\:\\\\stuff\\\\media");
newProperties.setProperty(
    "cddb.client",
    "AntelmannJavaCDDBReader");
newProperties.setProperty(
    "cddb.local.dir",
    "c\\:\\\\stuff\\\\misc\\\\cddb");
newProperties.setProperty("cddb.client.version", "0.4.0");

com.antelmann.util.Settings.init(newProperties);

try
{
    /*
 * This is where we use the Windows-specific native code to
 * read the CD information. To run this on other platforms
 * (e.g. Linux or Mac OS X) we'd need to provide a new
 * implementation of this.
 */
    com.antelmann.cddb.CDDriveWin myDrive =
        new com.antelmann.cddb.CDDriveWin( );

    /* Given the drive, we get the CD identification. */
    newCD.cdID = new com.antelmann.cddb.CDID(myDrive);

    /*
 * Next, we use the default FreeDB server to connect and
 * query for the available records.
 */
    com.antelmann.cddb.FreeDB myDB =
        new com.antelmann.cddb.FreeDB( );
    com.antelmann.cddb.CDDBRecord[] myRecords =
        myDB.queryCD(newCD.cdID);

    /*
 * For our purposes, we'll just accept the first record
 * that is returned and assume that it matches the inserted
 * CD.
 */
```

Example 9-3. Retrieving audio CD information (continued)

```
            com.antelmann.cddb.CDInfo myCDInfo =
                myDB.readCDInfo(myRecords[0]);

        /*
       * Now, we stuff the data using the standard parser into
       * the CD object.
       */
            newCD.cddbDetails =
                new com.antelmann.cddb.CDDBXmcdParser(
                    myCDInfo.getXmcdContent( ));

        } catch (Exception e)
        {
            e.printStackTrace( );
        }

    }

    public static void addAmazon(CD newCD)
    {
        try
        {
            AmazonSearchService myAmazonSearchService =
                new AmazonSearchServiceLocator( );
            AmazonSearchPort myAmazonSearchPort =
                myAmazonSearchService.getAmazonSearchPort( );

            ArtistRequest myArtistRequest = new ArtistRequest( );

            // Use this to set your Amazon Associates ID
            // For more info on Amazon Associates, see...
            // http://www.amazon.com/associates
            myArtistRequest.setTag(DeveloperTokens.amazon_associates);
            myArtistRequest.setDevtag(DeveloperTokens.amazon_token);

            // Here, we pass in the Artist as read by the CDDB results.
            myArtistRequest.setArtist(newCD.cddbDetails.readArtist( ));
            myArtistRequest.setLocale("us");
            myArtistRequest.setType("heavy");

            ProductInfo myProductInfo =
                myAmazonSearchPort.artistSearchRequest(myArtistRequest);

            // All we have to do now is loop through the Amazon
            // results, looking for a title that matches.
            Details[] myDetailsArray = myProductInfo.getDetails( );
            Details myDetail = null;
            for (int i = 0; i < myDetailsArray.length; i++)
                if (myDetailsArray != null)
                {
                    myDetail = myDetailsArray[i];
```

Example 9-3. Retrieving audio CD information (continued)

```
                    if (myDetail
                        .getProductName( )
                        .compareToIgnoreCase(
                            newCD.cddbDetails.readCDTitle( ))
                        == 0)
                        newCD.amazonDetails = myDetail;
            }
        } catch (Exception e)
        {
            e.printStackTrace( );
        }
    }

    public static CD addCD( )
    {
        CD newCD = new CD( );

        addCDDBInfo(newCD);
        addAmazon(newCD);

        cdList.put(newCD.cdID.getDiscID( ), newCD);

        return newCD;
    }

    private static Hashtable cdList = new Hashtable( );

    /**
     * An example of how the loaded data can be useful - here we loop
     * through the returned Amazon results, looking for the list price.
     * We add the results to a single total.
     */
    public static String getListValue( )
    {
        float value = 0;
        Enumeration list = cdList.keys( );
        while (list.hasMoreElements( ))
        {
            CD current = (CD)cdList.get(list.nextElement( ));
            if (current.amazonDetails != null)
                if (current.amazonDetails.getListPrice( ) != null)
                {
                    String valueString =
                        current.amazonDetails.getListPrice( );
                    valueString =
                        valueString.substring(1, valueString.length( ));

                    value = value + Float.parseFloat(valueString);
                }
        }
        return Float.toString(value);
    }
```

Example 9-3. Retrieving audio CD information (continued)

```java
public static java.util.Map getCDs()
{
    java.util.TreeMap map =
        new java.util.TreeMap(java.text.Collator.getInstance());

    Enumeration loop = cdList.keys();
    while (loop.hasMoreElements())
    {
        String key = (String)loop.nextElement();
        if (((CD)cdList.get(key)).cddbDetails != null)
            map.put(
                ((CD)cdList.get(key)).cddbDetails.readArtist(),
                cdList.get(key));
    }

    return map;
}

public static CD getCD(String id)
{
    return (CD)cdList.get(id);
}

public static void main(String[] args)
{
    CD myCD = addCD();
    System.out.println(myCD.cddbDetails.readArtist());
    System.out.println(myCD.amazonDetails.getAsin());
    System.out.println(myCD.getAmazonLink());
    System.out.println(myCD.amazonDetails.getImageUrlLarge());
    System.out.println(myCD.amazonDetails.getImageUrlMedium());
    System.out.println(myCD.amazonDetails.getImageUrlSmall());
    System.out.println(getListValue());
}
}
```

It's worth taking a moment to think about how much easier this was to accomplish by leveraging the com.antelmann classes rather than developing a custom library to access the CDDB data. Previous chapters have already shown interaction with FedEx, eBay, and PayPal, and the CDDB1 protocol is in some ways even more complex (not counting the native code needed to access the CD drive). We're lucky enough to be using a fairly popular programming language (Java). Imagine if you were interested in using the system using a nonmainstream language; you'd be forced to write a lot of code the Antelmann classes already provide for Java.

It's likely that if the designers of the CDDB set up the service today, they'd use a system closer to the WSDL plus SOAP methodology (or even XML-RPC). These systems make it much easier to generate the bridge glue (akin to the bulk of the com. antelmann.* classes) for individual programming languages. The other complexity—

that of the native code needed to access the CD drive—is one that lies beyond the realm of web services.

This is one more look at a web-service solution, provided this time by combining an existing library, a somewhat archaic protocol, and a modern SOAP interface to Amazon. A similar application might involve using a bar-code scanner to retrieve UPC codes and get competitive data from one or more web sites. Another example might use UPC code to instantly generate a used-item listing on eBay.

CHAPTER 10

Project 7: Hot News Sheet

If you're like me, you start your day by sitting down to work and opening a suite of web sites, trying to get a sense of what's going on in the world. In particular, I like to find both what's deemed popular by the mainstream media, as well the more democratic and populist views of the weblog community.

In this chapter, you'll build an application using RSS to provide a single web page showing what's hot from the mainstream news and the weblog universe, side by side. The application will additionally fold in results from a Google search on these topics for yet another angle on the news.

Presenting the News

One of the interesting things about this particular application is that it makes a series of calls to a number of servers, and, therefore, can easily take 15 to 20 seconds to completely populate the data from the various systems. This is far too long for any user to wait for a page to load (and indeed, most web browsers will time out after this long a delay). Therefore, when the application first starts, it displays a notice to the user, as shown in Figure 10-1. This notice is returned to the user immediately, and the news is fetched on another thread (in this case, using the built-in JDK java. util.TimerTask service).

As shown in Figure 10-2, after the data has been loaded, the viewer can see the results of the search. The main news stories as chosen by the Yahoo editorial team are displayed on the left. On the right, a feed retrieved from BlogDex (*http://blogdex. net/*) shows popular stories as determined by the weblog community.

Links providing easy access to pages with additional detail are shown in context. For example, links to reports with additional detail about the North Korean nuclear program are displayed next to the Yahoo news story. These links are based on data generated by Google search results.

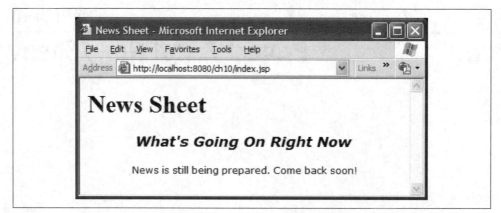

Figure 10-1. Waiting for the news

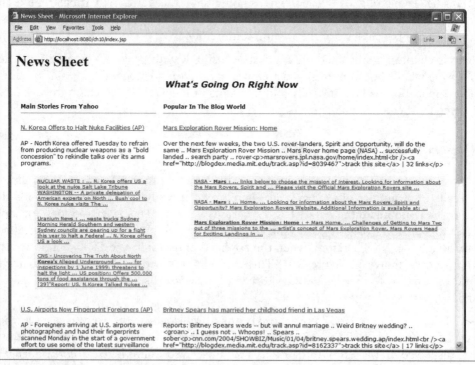

Figure 10-2. Viewing the news

As shown in Example 10-1, the bulk of the user interface is devoted to minimal formatting. The most important line, at the top, is the call to `NewsSheet.init()`; this verifies that the data is ready to be read. The remainder of the code is mostly concerned with looping through a set of returned data, formatted as `Story` objects.

Example 10-1. News JSP interface

```
<%@ page contentType="text/html; charset=iso-8859-1"
language="java" import="com.cascadetg.ch10.*" errorPage="" %>
<html>
<head>
<title>News Sheet</title>
·<meta http-equiv="Content-Type"
content="text/html; charset=iso-8859-1" />
<link href="../ch04/www/default.css" rel="stylesheet" type="text/css" />
</head>
<body>
<h1>News Sheet</h1>
<p align="center"><i><b><font size="+1">What's Going On Right Now</font></b></i></p>
<% if(!NewsSheet.init()) { %>
<p align="center">News is still being prepared. Come back soon!</p>
<% } else { %>

<table width="100%"  border="0" cellspacing="5" cellpadding="5">
  <tr>
    <td width="50%"><strong>Main Stories From Yahoo </strong>
    <hr /></td>
    <td width="50%"><strong>Popular In The Blog World </strong>
    <hr /></td>
  </tr>
<%
    for (int i = 0; i < 3; i++)
    {
%><tr>
<%
        for(int ii = 0; ii < 2; ii++)
        {
            Story current = NewsSheet.getStory(ii, i);
%>
    <td valign="top">
    <p><a target="_blank" href="<%=current.getLink( )%>"><%= current.getTitle( )%></a></p>
    <p><%= current.getDescription( )%></p>
<% if(ii != 2) { %>
<table width="90%"  border="0" align="right" cellpadding="3" cellspacing="3"
bgcolor="#FFFF99">
      <tr>
        <td>
          <%
            for(int x = 0; x < 3 ; x++)
            {
%>
          <p><small><a target="_blank" href="<%=current.getRelatedLink(x)%>"><%=
current.getRelatedTitle(x)%> : <%= current.getRelatedDescription(x)%></a><br />
          </small></p>
          <%
            }
%>
        </td>
      </tr>
```

Example 10-1. News JSP interface (continued)

```
    </table><% } %></td><%}%>
</tr><% } %>
</table>
<% } %>
</body>
</html>
```

The code shown in Example 10-2 serves as a data holder for the information returned by the various web services.

Example 10-2. Story data holder

```
package com.cascadetg.ch10;

public class Story
{
    protected String title = new String();
    protected String description = new String();
    protected String link = new String();

    protected String[] related_title = new String[3];
    protected String[] related_link = new String[3];
    protected String[] related_description = new String[3];

    public String getTitle()
    {
        return title;
    }

    public String getDescription()
    {
        return description;
    }

    public String getLink()
    {
        return link;
    }

    public String getRelatedTitle(int i)
    {
        return related_title[i];
    }

    public String getRelatedLink(int i)
    {
        return related_link[i];
    }

    public String getRelatedDescription(int i)
    {
```

Example 10-2. Story data holder (continued)

```
        return related_description[i];
    }
}
```

Gathering the News

The code in Example 10-3 performs the heavy lifting required to actually load the news. Notice that a URL to the PopDex service is included as well (but commented out). PopDex, *http://www.popdex.com/*, also provides feeds. Another popular service, DayPop (*http://www.daypop.com/*) offers a list of popular weblog memes. To add or change the feeds you're interested in (and therefore the content of the news service), simply include different RSS feed(s). For example, if you're interested in health issues, you might browse Yahoo's RSS offerings (*http://news.yahoo.com/rss*) for a more suitable, health-related feed.

Example 10-3. Building the news sheet

```
package com.cascadetg.ch10;

import java.util.Timer;

import de.nava.informa.core.ChannelIF;
import de.nava.informa.core.ItemIF;
import de.nava.informa.impl.basic.ChannelBuilder;
import de.nava.informa.parsers.RSSParser;
import com.google.soap.search.*;
import com.cascadetg.ch04.DeveloperTokens;

public class NewsSheet extends java.util.TimerTask
{
    static NewsSheet runner = null;
    public static boolean isReady = false;

    public static String blogdexURL =
        "http://blogdex.net/xml/index.asp";

    public static String popdexURL =
        "http://www.popdex.com/rss.xml";

    public static String yahooURL =
        "http://rss.news.yahoo.com/rss/topstories";

    public static Story[] yahooStories = new Story[3];
    public static Story[] blogdexStories = new Story[3];
//    public static Story[] popdexStories = new Story[3];

    public static String[] ignore_words =
        {
```

Example 10-3. Building the news sheet (continued)

```
            " the ",
            " to ",
            " for ",
            " of ",
            " and ",
            " a ",
            " as ",
            " in ",
            " on",
            "A ",
            "For ",
            "The ",
            "On ",
            "As ",
            "In " };

    public static Story getStory(int x, int y)
    {
        if (x == 0)
            return yahooStories[y];

        return blogdexStories[y];
        //return popdexStories[y];

    }

    static String stripCommon(String in)
    {
        String current = in;
        for (int i = 0; i < ignore_words.length; i++)
        {
            current = replaceToken(current, ignore_words[i], " ");
        }
        return current;
    }
```

As shown in the getGoogleResults() method at the start of Example 10-4, the request to Google strips the search term of common words before obtaining the search results. These common words (such as "and," "the," "of," etc.) are removed before sending the Google search string. By default, these words, called *stop words* in Google's parlance, are ignored. This word list is by no means definitive; most search engines (including Google) don't publish a stop-word list. Despite this, by excluding at least a known subset of these common stop words from counting against Google's 10 word limit, it increases the likelihood that the application will get an appropriate reference from Google's web service.

While this application removes words to ensure a better match, if the content for the site was more specific, the application could automatically include certain words in the search. For example, a Linux news site might include the word Linux in every search to help ensure that Google returns only relevant links.

Example 10-4. Building the news sheet, Part II

```
static GoogleSearchResultElement[] getGoogleResults(String in)
{
    String searchTerm = in;
    System.out.println(searchTerm);
    searchTerm = stripCommon(searchTerm);
    System.out.println(searchTerm);

    GoogleSearch search = new GoogleSearch( );

    // Set mandatory attributes
    search.setKey(DeveloperTokens.googleKey);
    search.setQueryString(searchTerm);

    // Set optional attributes
    search.setSafeSearch(true);
    // Invoke the actual search
    GoogleSearchResult result = null;
    try
    {
        result = search.doSearch( );
    } catch (GoogleSearchFault e)
    {
        e.printStackTrace( );
    }

    GoogleSearchResultElement[] mySearchElements =
        result.getResultElements( );

    return mySearchElements;
}

static void addGoogleToStory(Story story)
{
    GoogleSearchResultElement[] mySearchElements =
        getGoogleResults(story.title);

    for (int i = 0; i < story.related_title.length; i++)
    {
        if (i < mySearchElements.length)
        {
            story.related_title[i] = mySearchElements[i].getTitle( );
            String temp = mySearchElements[i].getSnippet( );
            temp = replaceToken(temp, "<b>", "");
            temp = replaceToken(temp, "</b>", "");
            temp = replaceToken(temp, "<br>", " ");
            story.related_description[i] = temp;
            story.related_link[i] = mySearchElements[i].getURL( );
        }
    }
}
```

Example 10-4. Building the news sheet, Part II (continued)

```java
static void addGoogleNotes(Story[] stories)
{
    for (int i = 0; i < stories.length; i++)
    {
        addGoogleToStory(stories[i]);
    }
}


static void refreshSiteStories(String feedURL, Story[] stories)
{
    try
    {
        java.net.URL inpFile = new java.net.URL(feedURL);
        ChannelIF channel =
            RSSParser.parse(new ChannelBuilder( ), inpFile);

        Object[] items = channel.getItems( ).toArray( );
        for (int i = 0; i < stories.length; i++)
        {
            stories[i] = new Story( );
            ItemIF current = (ItemIF)items[i];

            if (current.getTitle( ) != null)
                stories[i].title = current.getTitle( );

            if (current.getLink( ) != null)
                stories[i].link = current.getLink( ).toString( );

            if (current.getSubject( ) != null)
                if (current.getSubject( ).length( ) > 0)
                    System.out.println(
                        "#"
                        + (i + 1)
                        + " Subject"
                        + current.getSubject( ));

            if (current.getDescription( ) != null)
            {
                String temp = current.getDescription( );
                if (temp.length( ) > 1024)
                {
                    temp = temp.substring(0, 1020);
                    temp = temp + "...";
                }
                temp = replaceToken(temp, "<", "&lt;");
                temp = replaceToken(temp, ">", "&gt;");
                stories[i].description = temp;
            }

        }
    } catch (Exception e)
```

Example 10-4. Building the news sheet, Part II (continued)

```
    {
        e.printStackTrace( );
    }
    addGoogleNotes(stories);
}

public static void refreshStories( )
{
    long timing = System.currentTimeMillis( );

    refreshSiteStories(yahooURL, yahooStories);
    refreshSiteStories(blogdexURL, blogdexStories);
    //refreshSiteStories(popdexURL, popdexStories);
    System.out.println(System.currentTimeMillis( ) - timing);
    isReady = true;
}

public static void main(String[] args)
{
    while (!init( ))
    {
    }
    for (int i = 0; i < yahooStories.length; i++)
    {
        System.out.println("X" + yahooStories[i].title);
        System.out.println(
            "foo" + yahooStories[i].related_title[0]);
    }
    System.out.println("Program complete!");
}

/** All parameters must not be null. */
static public String replaceToken(
    String input,
    String token,
    String value)
{
    if (input == null)
        throw new NullPointerException(
        "replaceToken input should not be null");
    if (token == null)
        throw new NullPointerException(
        "replaceToken token should not be null");
    if (value == null)
        throw new NullPointerException(
        "replaceToken value should not be null");

    boolean done = false;
    int current = 0;
    int last = 0;
    StringBuffer results = new StringBuffer("");
    while (!done)
```

Example 10-4. Building the news sheet, Part II (continued)

```
        {
            last = current;
            current = input.indexOf(token, current);
            if (current == -1)
                done = true;
            if (!done)
            {
                results.append(input.substring(last, current));
                results.append(value);
                current = current + token.length();
            } else
            {
                results.append(input.substring(last));
            }
        }

        if (input.length() > 0)
            if (results.toString().length() == 0)
                return input;

        return results.toString();
    }

    public synchronized static boolean init()
    {
        if (runner == null)
        {
            runner = new NewsSheet();
            Timer myTimer = new Timer(true);
            myTimer.schedule(new NewsSheet(), 0, 1000L * 60L * 60L);
        }
        return isReady;
    }

    public void run()
    {
        System.out.print(
            new java.util.Date().toString() + "Refreshing...");

        refreshStories();
        System.out.println("Done");
    }

}
```

Notice that a couple of aspects of the code help you cope (at least partially) with the vagaries of RSS. For example, in the method addGoogleToStory( ), notice that the B and BR tags Google inserts into the search summary are stripped out. Google places these tags into their response consistently, regardless of your needs. Similarly, while Yahoo offers a very "pure" feed—only plain text is sent in their article—the stories as selected by BlogDex typically contain all sorts of odd formatting. For example, in the screenshot shown in Figure 10-2, notice that the right column is significantly wider than the left column; this is due to a long URL with no breaks or spaces in one of the feeds. As touched on in the previous chapter, writing a parser engine that can handle every bizarre idea of an RSS file can quickly become an exercise in frustration.

As you can see, RSS (and Google search) are powerful tools for enhancing a site; these provide for inexpensive but interesting access to content. Despite the limitations of RSS, it's easy to see the power of aggregation for a reader (and publisher) of content. Intelligent automation can go a long way toward providing useful content.

CHAPTER 11

Project 8: Automatic Daily Discussions

Let's say that you decide to set up a weblog covering the latest news on Java and XML programming. You'd like to keep it fresh, ideally posting new content every day to spur conversations. Finally, you want new content to be posted automatically—even if you're away. We know that Google is constantly indexing the Web, culling out undesirables, and doing everything it can to deliver useful results for specific searches. Why not leverage that search capability to find out interesting topics for conversation in a community?

In this chapter, you'll build an application to combine your Blogger (*http://www. blogger.com/*) or LiveJournal (*http://www.livejournal.com/*) weblog with Google's search functionality.

Weblogs

A *weblog* is a web site with a set of stories, sorted chronologically. Generally speaking, the idea is that it should be extremely easy to post a new story to a weblog, allowing for very natural, seamless writing. Personal weblogs often resemble diaries or journals. Group or corporate weblogs typically serve to allow a group of people with common interests to share thoughts, news, or discuss problems.

The precise definition of a weblog varies. Similarly, there's a huge variety in the software used to run and manage a weblog. Some, like LiveJournal and Blogger, are hosted on a central server. Others are desktop software, and still others are installed on individual personal web servers. There are distinct advantages and disadvantages to each model. For example, LiveJournal offers a "friends" feature that allows you to mark entries as private and only viewable by users on your friends list. Because friends are in turn registered users (i.e., they all have their own journals), it's easy to see how LiveJournal quickly became a popular site. At the other end of the spectrum, desktop software, such as Radio UserLand (*http://radio.userland.com/*), allows tremendous customization and lets you write posts even if you aren't connected to the Internet.

UserLand was one of the first systems to offer a web service that interfaces with weblogs—born in part out of a desire to offer a scripting system that relied on standard TCP/IP and networking standards instead of proprietary, single-platform systems. The original, pre-SOAP system is known as XML-RPC (*http://www.xmlrpc. com/*, a site hosted by UserLand).

XML-RPC and Weblogs

XML-RPC is SOAP's stripped down, lighter-weight predecessor. For example, there is no such thing as WSDL in XML-RPC. Instead, developers interested in working with XML-RPC rely on the provided documentation and XML-RPC libraries for their preferred language. Because this application is built with Java, it uses the Apache XML-RPC libraries available from *http://ws.apache.org/xmlrpc/* (shown in Figure 11-1).

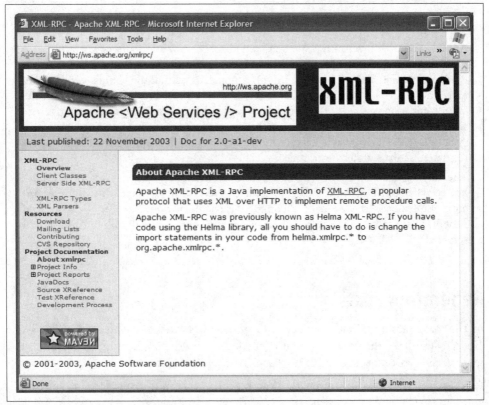

Figure 11-1. Apache XML-RPC web site

XML-RPC merely provides the mechanism for making a call to a remote server; it doesn't specify anything else about the service. This means that for each system you wish to connect to, you must read and understand the API documentation:

- LiveJournal (*http://www.livejournal.com/doc/server/ljp.csp.xml-rpc.protocol.html*)
- Blogger (*http://new.blogger.com/developers/api/1_docs/*)

These APIs are pretty different, but as will be shown in this chapter, a single application can address both systems. To isolate the details of the underlying vendor-specific weblog web-service interfaces from the rest of the application's functionality, an interface is used that describes posting a weblog entry in a generic fashion (in some ways, this is analogous to a generic driver interface providing interfaces to multiple data sources). The sample application in this chapter accesses two implementations—one for Blogger and one for LiveJournal.

What About Atom?

As of this writing, LiveJournal, Blogger, and many other weblog software creators have pledged support to a single, unified new weblog API and syndication format (*http://www.intertwingly.net/wiki/pie/RoadMap*). The idea is that all the various vendors will agree to a single API (replacing the Blogger and LiveJournal APIs, as well as all of the others) and a single syndication format (replacing the various RSS incarnations). A nice side benefit of this is that by ensuring that the API and the syndication format are in sync, it'll make it easier to integrate the two (for example, the API could return data formatted in the syndication format).

The only downside of Atom is that the specification isn't complete, nor is there a timeline for when it will be. Until then, you'll have to rely on an interface with multiple concrete implementations to handle connecting to the various services. When Atom support is available, you'll be able to a use a new, single class to talk to Atom-based services.

Generating Posts

In this case, a standalone application with a standard main( ) method will talk to Google and make the posts. All that is needed to run the application is to launch the main class, com.cascadetg.ch11.PostGenerator, with no arguments.

As shown in the code starting with Example 11-1, the built-in Java facility for timers (java.util.Timer) generates the posts on a regular schedule. The main loop just sits idle. It's easy to imagine incorporating this application into another application, such as a desktop client weblog application.

Example 11-1's application uses the Amazon web service connectivity as shown in Chapter 4, as well a single utility method (NewsSheet.replaceToken( )) from Chapter 11.

Example 11-1. Generating posts

```java
package com.cascadetg.ch11;

import java.util.Date;
import java.util.Hashtable;
import java.util.Timer;
import com.google.soap.search.*;
import com.cascadetg.ch04.DeveloperTokens;
import com.cascadetg.ch10.NewsSheet;

public class PostGenerator extends java.util.TimerTask
{

    /**
     * These constants are used to describe the frequency at which
     * posts should be made
     */
    static final long MINUTE = 60L * 1000L;
    static final long HOUR = 60L * 60L * 1000L;
    static final long DAY = 24L * 60L * 60L * 1000L;
    static final long WEEK = 7L * 24L * 60L * 60L * 1000L;

    /**
     * The defined frequency. For a "real" system, you'd likely want to
     * set this to DAY - MINUTE is only appropriate for debugging (and
     * some vendors have implemented policies that won't allow for
     * sustained posts at this frequency.
     */
    long frequency = MINUTE;

    /**
     * This Hashtable is used to store the list of URLs that we have
     * retrieved from Google and (at least tried) to post. In the real
     * world, you'd want to persist this to a database.
     */
    Hashtable postedStories = new Hashtable( );

    /**
     * This is the search term we'll be sending to Google as the basis
     * for our posts.
     */
    String search_term;

    /** This is used to specify the weblog we will be posting to. */
    WeblogDriverInterface weblog;
```

Example 11-1. Generating posts (continued)

```
public static void main(String[] args)
{
    PostGenerator myPoster = new PostGenerator( );

    // This is where we choose which weblog we will be posting to.
    myPoster.setWeblog(new LiveJournalDriver( ));
    // myPoster.setWeblog(new BloggerDriver( ));

    myPoster.setSearchTerm("Java XML");
    myPoster.init( );

    // This is just a dummy loop which allows the program to run
    // for a while before exiting.
    boolean done = false;
    while (!done)
    {
        try
        {
            Thread.sleep(1000L * 10L);
        } catch (Exception e)
        {
            e.printStackTrace( );
        }
    }
    System.out.println("Program complete.");
}
```

The retrieval of data from Google's search web service is performed by the
getGoogleResults( ) method in Example 11-2. The returned data is formatted into a
human-readable post (with some light HTML formatting) in the getGoogleStory( )
method. You may wish to provide some additional logic for your own site; for example, you might write five different bits of text introducing the search results and
rotate between them to keep the site fresh.

Example 11-2. Generating posts, Part II

```
/** Uses the Google web service interface to get the search results */
GoogleSearchResultElement[] getGoogleResults( )
{
    GoogleSearch search = new GoogleSearch( );

    // Set mandatory attributes
    search.setKey(DeveloperTokens.googleKey);
    search.setQueryString(search_term);

    // Set optional attributes
    search.setSafeSearch(true);

    // Invoke the actual search
    GoogleSearchResult result = null;
    try
```

Example 11-2. Generating posts, Part II (continued)

```
        {
            result = search.doSearch( );
        } catch (GoogleSearchFault e)
        {
            e.printStackTrace( );
        }

        GoogleSearchResultElement[] mySearchElements =
            result.getResultElements( );

        return mySearchElements;
    }

    /**
     * Gets the search results, loops through them, finds a result that
     * hasn't been posted yet, formats, and then returns the discussion
     * text as a single formatted HTML string.
     */
    String getGoogleStory( )
    {
        StringBuffer post = new StringBuffer( );

        GoogleSearchResultElement[] mySearchElements =
            getGoogleResults( );

        for (int i = 0; i < mySearchElements.length; i++)
        {
            if (!postedStories
                .containsKey(mySearchElements[i].getURL( )))
            {
                post.append("As of ");
                post.append(new Date( ).toLocaleString( ));
                post.append(" Google thinks that ");
                post.append(" <a href='");
                post.append(mySearchElements[i].getURL( ));
                post.append("' target='_blank'>this website");
                post.append("</a> on '");
                post.append(mySearchElements[i].getTitle( ));
                post.append("' is a relevant to ");
                post.append(search_term);
                post.append(". <BR /><BR /><I>");
                post.append(mySearchElements[i].getSummary( ));
                post.append(" ");

                post.append(
                    NewsSheet.replaceToken(
                        mySearchElements[i].getSnippet( ),
                        "<br>",
                        " "));
                post.append("</I><BR /><BR /> What do you think?");
```

Example 11-2. Generating posts, Part II (continued)

```
                postedStories.put(
                    mySearchElements[i].getURL( ),
                    new java.util.Date( ));

                return post.toString( );
            }
        }

        String defaultString =
            "It would seem that Google can't find "
            + "anything new on the topic "
            + search_term
            + ". Why do you think that is?";

        return defaultString;
    }
```

As shown in Example 11-3, the code for generating the post generates them at regular intervals. A simple java.util.Timer invokes the task and thereby generates a post on a regular frequency. The remainder of the class is concerned with bookkeeping.

Example 11-3. Generating posts, Part III

```
/**
 * This method takes the formatted text from the Google search and
 * then generates a post.
 */
public void makePost( )
{
    String postText = getGoogleStory( );
    java.util.Date now = new Date( );
    weblog.setPost(postText);
    weblog.setTitle(
        "Discussion Topic for "
            + (now.getMonth( ) + 1)
            + "/"
            + now.getDate( ));
    if (!weblog.post( ))
    {
        System.out.println("Unable to make post.");
    } else
    {
        System.out.println("Post made.");
    }
}

/** Sets up the timer for this object. */
public synchronized void init( )
{
```

Example 11-3. Generating posts, Part III (continued)

```
        Timer myTimer = new Timer(true);
        myTimer.schedule(this, 0, frequency);
    }

    /**
     * The required method by the Timer interface. This method is
     * triggered as indicated by the Timer thread.
     */
    public void run( )
    {
        System.out.print(
            new java.util.Date( ).toString( ) + " refreshing...");

        makePost( );
        System.out.println("Done");
    }

    // The remainder of this class is the usual JavaBean
    // getters/setters.
    public WeblogDriverInterface getWeblog( )
    {
        return weblog;
    }

    public void setWeblog(WeblogDriverInterface weblog)
    {
        this.weblog = weblog;
    }

    public void setSearchTerm(String search)
    {
        search_term = search;

    }

    public String getSearchTerm( )
    {
        return search_term;
    }
}
```

The code shown in Example 11-4 shows how a weblog is presented to the post generation class. Two standard JavaBean-style properties set the post title and content, and a single post( ) method submits the post to the weblog.

Example 11-4. Weblog driver interface

```
package com.cascadetg.ch11;

public interface WeblogDriverInterface
{
```

Example 11-4. Weblog driver interface (continued)

```
    String getPost();
    void setPost(String post);

    String getTitle();
    void setTitle(String title);

    /** Return true if the post is successful, false if not */
    boolean post();
}
```

Generating a LiveJournal Post

Example 11-5 shows how a connection can be made to the LiveJournal service. Notice that a MD5 hashed version of the journal password is passed to the system: it's not a significant security aid, but it's slightly better than nothing.

The LiveJournal connection emulates a named parameter method invocation, closer to the named-pair values you see in HTTP parameters. This is done by passing an XML-RPC struct. One advantage of this approach is that the arguments do not have to be passed in any specific order, which makes it easier to build and also easier to debug.

Example 11-5. LiveJournal connectivity

```
package com.cascadetg.ch11;

import org.apache.xmlrpc.*;

import java.util.Hashtable;
import java.util.Vector;

public class LiveJournalDriver implements WeblogDriverInterface
{

    public static void main(String[] args)
    {
        LiveJournalDriver myDriver = new LiveJournalDriver();
        myDriver.setPost("Test @ " + new java.util.Date().toString());
        myDriver.setPost("Foo!");
        System.out.println("LiveJournal test " + myDriver.post());
    }

    String post;
    public void setPost(String post)
    {
        this.post = post;
    }
```

Example 11-5. LiveJournal connectivity (continued)

```java
public String getPost( )
{
    return post;
}

String title = "";
public String getTitle( )
{
    return title;
}

public void setTitle(String title)
{
    this.title = title;
}

/** Post to LiveJournal using the LJ-specific XML-RPC interface. */
public boolean post( )
{
    /*
     * Note that we are using a utility class to send the password
     * encrypted as an MD5 hash. This isn't much in the way of
     * security - all it means is that if intercepted, the
     * intercepter will get a hashed version of the password, not
     * the original plain-text version.
     */
    String password = MD5Hash.hash(BlogTokens.livejournal_password);
    Hashtable method_calls = new Hashtable( );

    try
    {
        String lj_url =
            "http://www.livejournal.com/interface/xmlrpc";
        XmlRpcClient xmlrpc = new XmlRpcClient(lj_url);
        Vector params = new Vector( );

        method_calls.put(
            "username",
            BlogTokens.livejournal_username);
        method_calls.put(
            "password",
            BlogTokens.livejournal_password);
        method_calls.put("ver", "1");
        method_calls.put("clientversion", "WebServiceBook/0.0.1");
        java.util.Date now = new java.util.Date( );
        method_calls.put("event", post);
        method_calls.put("lineendings", "\n");
        method_calls.put("subject", title);
        method_calls.put("year", new Integer(now.getYear( ) + 1900));
        method_calls.put("mon", new Integer(now.getMonth( ) + 1));
        method_calls.put("day", new Integer(now.getDate( )));
        method_calls.put("hour", new Integer(now.getHours( )));
```

Example 11-5. LiveJournal connectivity (continued)

```
        method_calls.put("min", new Integer(now.getMinutes()));

        params.add(method_calls);

        Object result =
            xmlrpc.execute("LJ.XMLRPC.postevent", params);
    } catch (Exception e)
    {
        e.printStackTrace();
        return false;
    }
    return true;
    }
}
```

Figure 11-2 shows an example of a post made to the LiveJournal site. The template chosen for the LiveJournal account determines the design and format of the post.

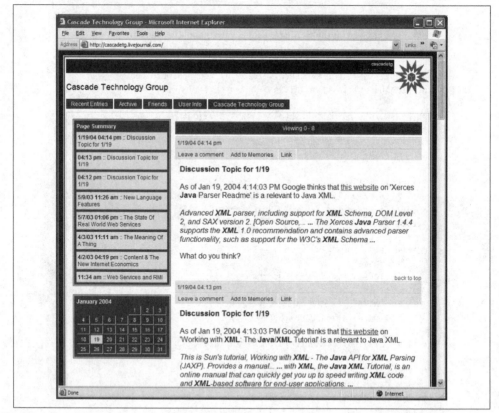

Figure 11-2. LiveJournal generated post

Example 11-6 shows how to make a post to the Blogger. The only potential area of confusion is that the parameters must be provided in the order shown. The biggest weakness of this API is the lack of a mechanism to specify the title of the post.

The Blogger 1.0 API does not include any mechanism for posting entries to Blogger with a title. Blogger did some work on a Blogger 2.0 API, but this was dropped in favor of Atom. The Blogger 2.0 API did include a mechanism for sending a post with a title, but Blogger has officially discontinued efforts on the Blogger 2.0 effort. Blogger has left a preliminary Blogger 2.0 API implementation active as of this writing, but it's impossible to tell when that functionality will disappear.

Aside from the missing title parameter, the Blogger API in Example 11-6 is quite straightforward.

Example 11-6. Blogger connectivity

```
package com.cascadetg.ch11;

import org.apache.xmlrpc.*;

import java.util.Vector;

public class BloggerDriver implements WeblogDriverInterface
{

    public static void main(String[] args)
    {
        BloggerDriver myDriver = new BloggerDriver();
        myDriver.setPost("Test @ " + new java.util.Date().toString());
        System.out.println("Blogger test " + myDriver.post());
    }

    /**
     * Note that the Blogger XML-RPC interface does not support setting
     * the title of a post, so this is only provided to adhere to the
     * expected behavior for this pattern as required by the interface.
     */
    private String title = "";
    public String getTitle()
    {
        return title;
    }
    public void setTitle(String title)
    {
        this.title = title;
    }

    String body;
    public void setPost(String post)
    {
```

Example 11-6. Blogger connectivity (continued)

```
        this.body = post;
    }

    public String getPost( )
    {
        return body;
    }

    /**
     * Makes the post to the Blogger interface using the Blogger 1.0
     * XML-RPC interface.
     */
    public boolean post( )
    {
        String url = "http://plant.blogger.com/api/RPC2";

        try
        {
            XmlRpcClient xmlrpc = new XmlRpcClient(url);
            Vector params = new Vector( );

            params.add(BlogTokens.blogger_app_key);
            params.add(BlogTokens.blogger_blogid);
            params.add(BlogTokens.blogger_username);
            params.add(BlogTokens.blogger_password);
            params.add(body);
            params.add(Boolean.TRUE);

            Object result = xmlrpc.execute("blogger.newPost", params);
        } catch (Exception e)
        {
            e.printStackTrace( );
            return false;
        }
        return true;

    }
}
```

To change the system to use the Blogger driver instead of LiveJournal, merely comment out the line for LiveJournal and uncomment the Blogger line, in your code from Example 11-1:

```
// This is where we choose which weblog we will be posting to.
// myPoster.setWeblog(new LiveJournalDriver( ));
myPoster.setWeblog(new BloggerDriver( ));
```

Viewing the Blogger Post

You can see the results of a post to the Blogger weblog system in Figure 11-3.

Figure 11-3. Blogger-generated post

Similar to LiveJournal, the actual display and formatting of the posts is governed by the Blogger templates.

For completeness, Example 11-7 shows a utility class that assists with converting a string to an MD5 hash, as used in the LiveJournal access code. An MD5 hash is a one-way hash; it allows you to discover a unique "fingerprint" of a lump of text without being able to recover the original string. It's commonly used to store passwords in a database, for example.

Example 11-7. MD5 hash example

```
package com.cascadetg.ch11;
import java.security.*;

public class MD5Hash
{

    /**
     * Private function to turn md5 result into a properly formatted 32
     * hex-digit string
     */
    private static String asHex(byte hash[])
    {
```

Example 11-7. MD5 hash example (continued)

```java
        StringBuffer temp = new StringBuffer(hash.length * 2);
        int i;

        for (i = 0; i < hash.length; i++)
        {
            if ((hash[i] & 0xff) < 0x10)
                temp.append("0");

            temp.append(Long.toString(hash[i] & 0xff, 16));
        }

        return temp.toString( );
    }

    /**
     * Take a string and return its md5 hash as a hex digit string
     */
    public static String hash(String arg)
    {
        return hash(arg.getBytes( ));
    }

    /**
     * Take a byte array and return its md5 hash as a hex digit string
     */
    public static String hash(byte barray[])
    {
        Provider[] providers = java.security.Security.getProviders( );
        Provider myProvider = null;

        for (int i = 0; i < providers.length; i++)
        {
            if (providers[i].getName( ).compareTo("SUN") == 0)
            {
                myProvider = providers[i];
            }
        }

        if (myProvider == null)
        {
            return "Unable to load Sun security package";
        }

        MessageDigest md = null;
        try
        {
            md = MessageDigest.getInstance("MD5");
        } catch (java.security.NoSuchAlgorithmException e)
        {
            return "Unable to load Sun security provider";
        }
```

Example 11-7. MD5 hash example (continued)

```
        md.update(barray);

        return asHex(md.digest( ));
    }
}
```

Finally, as shown in Example 11-8, you must enter the username and password for your preferred service.

Example 11-8. Weblog tokens

```
package com.cascadetg.ch11;

public class BlogTokens
{
    /* LiveJournal tokens */
    static public String livejournal_username = "username";
    static public String livejournal_password = "secret_password";

    /* Blogger tokens */
    static public String blogger_app_key =
        "01234567890123456789012345678901"
            + "12345678901234567890123456789012"
            + "12345678901234567890123456789012";

    static public String blogger_blogid = "1234567";
    static public String blogger_username = "other_username";
    static public String blogger_password = "other_password";
}
```

A weblog provides an efficient and simple way to integrate content. The formatting and design are separate from the content. A simple web service interface allows one system to generate content and post it in an automated fashion to another.

We've seen that much of the work to be done with web services is really a question of system integration. The final chapter ponders what this means for web services, and what the future of web services may look like.

CHAPTER 12

Future Web Service Directions

Throughout this text, you've seen a variety of different web services and technologies for connecting to web services. At some point, this wide array of options will transition from the interesting to the onerous. As of this writing, SOAP and WSDL are enjoying broad adoptions (e.g., both eBay and PayPal have released SOAP/WSDL interfaces).

This chapter first describes some of the more futuristic web service technologies, including REST, UDDI, Rendezvous, and BPEL/BPEL4WS. Then, based on the information in the book, we'll look at the future of web service development, considering ease-of-use, the need for a business model, security, and finally a way to consider the consolidation of web services.

Future Technologies

The number of technologies lumped with web services is often overwhelming. In this section, I'll describe REST, cited by some as an alternative to SOAP, the UDDI registry; local service registration with Rendezvous; and touch briefly on BPEL.

REST

Representational State Transfer (REST) is a SOAP alternative. An elegant description of REST can be found at *http://www.xfront.com/REST-Web-Services.html*:

> Representational State Transfer is intended to evoke an image of how a well-designed Web application behaves: a network of web pages (a virtual state-machine), where the user progresses through an application by selecting links (state transitions), resulting in the next page (representing the next state of the application) being transferred to the user and rendered for their use.

> —Roy Fielding
> *http://www.ics.uci.edu/%7Efielding/pubs/webarch_*
> *icse2000.pdf*

In practice, REST simply refers to a mechanism with which you pass a request query and receive an XML document in response. As you've seen, this is likely to lead to extensive code that can parse these documents. In the Java case, this means writing Java objects to help work with XML documents. Using Axis and WSDL, you (or the API vendor) can automatically generate this bridge code.

That said, informal sources point to broader adoption of REST versus SOAP. Amazon offers both REST and SOAP interfaces. Indeed, there are reports that as much as 85% of the traffic using Amazon's web services is based on REST instead of SOAP (*http://www.oreillynet.com/pub/wlg/3005*). Unfortunately, if the examples as shown in this book are any indication, REST-based projects are liable to lead to considerably more client code for the maintenance of the XML processing as compared to SOAP-based solutions.

UDDI

One of the specifications often associated with web services is Universal Description, Discovery and Integration (UDDI). You can learn more about UDDI at *http://www.uddi.org/* and find additional services at *http://www.uddi.org/find.html*.

UDDI offers a system for discovery based on a developer browsing a registry. There has been some talk of allowing dynamic discovery of web services, but little agreement and little in the way of broadly accepted implementations. Figure 12-1 shows the basic model: a centralized UDDI server is responsible for the location of clients. While the theory sounds nice, in practice there are few services that seem to use this system. As we've seen, few services use even SOAP and WSDL, and UDDI is a relatively complex system with relatively little apparent benefit for the complexity presented.

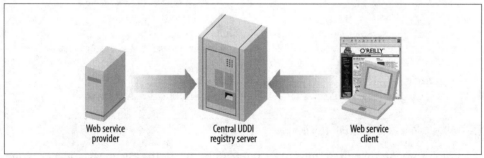

Figure 12-1. UDDI discovery model

A somewhat more human-palatable version of the UDDI registry is presented by the services afforded by *http://www.bindingpoint.com/* and *http://www.xmethods.net/*.

As shown in Figure 12-2, you can see a variety of web services broken up along various categories. As of this writing, the categories (and the services listed) are broken up as shown in Figure 12-3.

Figure 12-2. BindingPoint web site

Business & Economy (199)
Accounts , Finance , Parcel Delivery ...

Graphics (13)

Calendar (18)

Other (392)
Demonstrations , Games , Test Services

Communications (83)
Collaboration , Email , Fax ...

Reference (107)
Address Information , Web Service Discovery

Content (75)
Daily Information , Jokes , News ...

Utilities (136)
Conversion , Encryption , Mathematics

Figure 12-3. BindingPoint category listings

It's not surprising that the majority of the listings are in the Business and Economy section. We've covered some of the top rated web services in this book, including Amazon and Interfax's fax service. Others are less useful—for example, a joke-of-the-day service.

The difficult thing about measuring the success of "web services" is that for any given service, there's no way to track the total number of users. So, if there are 10 major web services (for example, the ones described in this book) and another 200 or

300 trivial ones, but the major ones are used by tens of thousands of developers, does that count as success?

The XMethods web site (Figure 12-4), in addition to free system for registering web services, offers a useful WSDL validation utility at *http://www.xmethods.net/ve2/ Tools.po*. You can see the results of the validation utility when pointed at Amazon's WSDL file (*http://soap.amazon.com/schemas3/AmazonWebServices.wsdl*) in Figure 12-5.

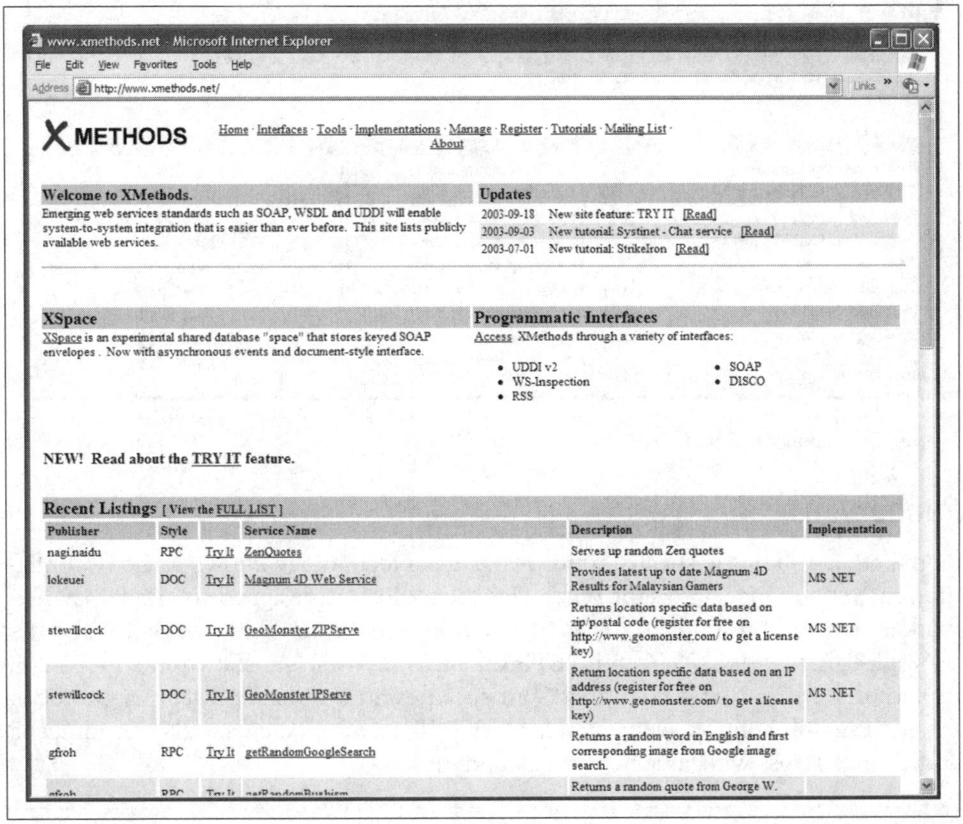

Figure 12-4. XMethods web site

As you can see, this is a useful exploratory tool and shows the importance of WSDL for tools and mechanical "self-disclosure" of web services.

Despite this functionality, UDDI has not enjoyed broad public adoption, despite tremendous and vocal support from a variety of vendors over a period of several years. Most web service vendors seem content to publish a WSDL URI on a web site in lieu of a UDDI infrastructure.

Service Binding - Microsoft Internet Explorer

File Edit View Favorites Tools Help

Address http://www.xmethods.net/ve2/WSDLAnalyzer.po

✗METHODS

WSDL Analyzer : Operations

for the WSDL file http://soap.amazon.com/schemas3/AmazonWebServices.wsdl

The following table lists the operations for the service. You can drill down into the various messages associated with the operations by clicking on the message links.

Operation / Method Name	SOAPAction*	Style	Input Message
KeywordSearchRequest	http://soap.amazon.com	rpc	Input Msg
TextStreamSearchRequest	http://soap.amazon.com	rpc	Input Msg
PowerSearchRequest	http://soap.amazon.com	rpc	Input Msg
BrowseNodeSearchRequest	http://soap.amazon.com	rpc	Input Msg
AsinSearchRequest	http://soap.amazon.com	rpc	Input Msg
BlendedSearchRequest	http://soap.amazon.com	rpc	Input Msg
UpcSearchRequest	http://soap.amazon.com	rpc	Input Msg
SkuSearchRequest	http://soap.amazon.com	rpc	Input Msg
AuthorSearchRequest	http://soap.amazon.com	rpc	Input Msg

Figure 12-5. Amazon WSDL analyzed

Rendezvous

At the other end of the spectrum from UDDI is a technology known as Zero Configuration Networking, or "ZeroConf." This technology is designed to allow easy network access and browsing via TCP/IP networks (similar to the browsing capabilities of AppleTalk for Mac OS X and NETBIOS on Windows). As shown in Figure 12-6, in lieu of a centralized server, ZeroConf specifies an automatic discovery protocol. Clients can still connect using standard TCP/IP services (such as DNS or direct IP addressing) across wide area network boundaries.

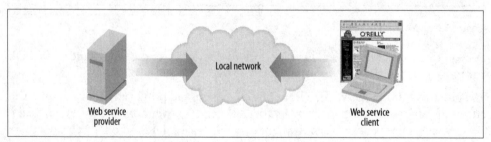

Figure 12-6. ZeroConf discovery model

Apple bundles ZeroConf technology as a core part of Mac OS X under the name Rendezvous. It's used in a variety of areas—for example, discovering local web sites in the Safari web browser, finding local chat and videoconferencing systems with iChat, finding printers, and even connecting your Mac OS X system to your TiVo without complex configuration.

For Java developers, it's easy to add support for discovering ZeroConf/Rendezvous services using the library at *http://jmdns.sourceforge.net/*. The library is still in an early stage, but it does offer a glimpse of a possible future direction for web services. It provides a simple way for a "server" application to broadcast the connection point for a set of SOAP interfaces, and if a listening "client" knows about the provided interface, it can communicate using SOAP interfaces.

At a human level, this is almost obvious; it's easy to imagine a work group in which systems and services appear and are immediately useful and necessary, but small failures are more or less inconsequential. Consider, for example, a peer-to-peer file sharing application or chat application. If the system fails, you have a simple, informal fall-back system, in large part based on the human interaction. Conversely, larger scale business processes require trust and a high bar for discovery and integration. If you want to purchase a large number of components to build a product for commercial sale, you're going to have a lot of requirements in terms of quality,

BPEL/BPEL4WS

Business Process Expression Language (BPEL), describes a process that accesses multiple synchronous and asynchronous web services given WSDL. The original submitters for BPEL were IBM, Microsoft, and BEA, so it's likely we'll see support for the these vendors. In addition, Collaxa has done significant work around BPEL and BPEL4WS (BPEL for Web Services). In addition to their products, a tutorial can be found at *http://www.collaxa.com/developer.bpel101.html*. That said, it's difficult to find much in the way of concrete support or interest for BPEL/BPEL4WS.

Future Directions

In this section, I'll look at some of the larger issues facing web services, including the complexity of development, the need for a business model, security, and finally present a mental model for tracking the evolution of web services over the near future.

Lowering the Bar

In this text, we've focused on Java as our development language of choice. Over time, a variety of scripting languages have appeared, promising to broaden the range of programming and development to a wider audience. Many vendors of development tools talk of a three-tiered model, with "ordinary users," "scripters," and "software developers" occupying the three ranks. Sometimes, this is broken down as "HTML," "scripting," "procedural," and "object-oriented" development.

In some ways, it would be more accurate to break down the complexity of web service development along the lines of client development and server development. This text has focused almost exclusively on client development—not web service server development. Applications may function as a server relative to the user's web browser, but we have not attempted to provide our own web services (save for an RSS feed).

As the component model for web application development matures, it's possible that the use of the more complex web service infrastructure such as SOAP and WSDL will be sufficiently encapsulated so as to make the development of web service applications accessible via visual builder tools. For example, several commercial tools now available allow a user to specify a WSDL and automatically generate web service components.

Understanding the Business Model

Almost all of the web services offered by various companies are provided for free in conjunction with an offline service of some kind. For example, FedEx provides the web services for free, but they charge to actually ship something. Similarly, Amazon offers free web services (indeed, they pay for you to publish material using their associates program), but they charge to actually ship products.

An open question is the viability of charging for web service access in and of itself. For example, eBay keeps track of the overall usage of the web services system and charges fees based on the access. In practice, this means that eBay is charging auction fees and also fees to view and post auctions. It's unlikely that eBay would have been successful if had applied a per-page-fee formula to ordinary web browsing.

This is very important and very significant for the future of the Internet. For example, an inexpensive pay-per-access web service model could pave the way for a micropayment system for access to content and software. Alternatively, it could also provide for richer integration between a client and a server for specific applications.

It introduces the potential for a richer economic model between a publisher of a service and desktop software. For example, a vendor that sells music online might offer a set of interfaces to access the system. The makers of desktop software could then create new clients to access the system with different capabilities, obtaining a commission for music sold through the system. In this fashion, a richer economic model is created, with more customer choice.

To date, this has been limited by the tendency of a corporation to want to own the entire chain of experience between themselves and the end user. This is the difference between the vendor of an application or a point product and a platform.

Security

Security in web services is still a somewhat mixed system. Throughout this text, we've seen a variety of approaches, and this variety is likely to continue for some time. Some services support HTTPS- and SSL-based connection encryption. A minor gesture is made toward security with the use of an MD5 hash for passing along passwords. There are a variety of tokens required to access different systems. At minimum, the following are all required to access a service: a single developer token, an authentication token, an application token, a user account, and a password.

It's easy to criticize the efforts with regard to security that have been made, but one of the biggest advantages of web services is the very reliance on the underlying standards. For higher security environments, it's easy to envision using existing technologies such as SSH or a VPN. Proxy servers and services can provide for robust logging and debugging capability. The same XML that SOAP relies on makes it easy for a proxy system to inspect the messages being sent.

Consolidation

The wide availability of SOAP clients and servers and the broad industry support from both small and large vendors is a very positive sign. XML-RPC also enjoys wide support, and the simplicity and stability of the specification mean that many of the libraries used are also stable. RSS also enjoys widespread support, but the sheer variety of feeds and the various "interpretations" of the specification make it much harder to work with than one might hope.

Interestingly, all of these rely on XML. There is a rich tradition of text-based protocols underlying the Internet, and XML allows a developer to provide a text-based representation without having to write a parser (one of the nastier, more error-prone pieces of software one can write). Even REST, one of the more aggressive alternative approaches, relies on XML as a primary data type.

The bright side is that virtually all vendors have agreed on XML as a universal glue. With the exception of CDDB, every service in this book uses XML in some fashion. It's likely that all these systems are going to move along a more or less predictable axis toward SOAP and WSDL as the developers of both the client and server side of the software get tired of reinventing the wheel. For example, why bother constantly recreating binding layers between your preferred development language and your server when simply standardizing on SOAP and WSDL gives you multilanguage bindings "for free?" Indeed, many systems automatically provide WSDL bindings automatically when you build a SOAP service.

Figure 12-7 attempts to capture the "evolution" of systems as they move from a more closed, binary system to a more mature, open, pure web services model. It's extremely trivial for most development systems to render a binary data file or push binary data "across the wire." This is almost useless for a web service model, as few developers have the time or inclination to support a specific, binary interface. It's difficult to maintain, and more often than not requires locking both the service provider and the clients into a potentially very fragile system.

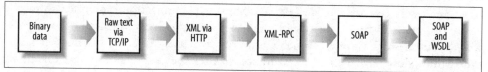

Figure 12-7. Web service openness and maturity

The next stage, raw (or very loosely formatted) text, typically piped over TCP/IP, is much easier to work with than a binary format. Prior to the popularity of XML, this was the de facto standard for virtually all Internet protocols. FTP, HTTP, NNTP, Gopher, SMTP, MIME are all based on specific text markers for delimiting data. For example, if you browse through the IETF site and looking at the original specification for HTTP (at *http://www.ietf.org/rfc/rfc1945.txt?number=1945*), you'll notice that tremendous attention is paid to low level detail (the same sort of detail and Backus-Naur Form [BNF] grammar rules that one might expect from a compiler specification). The Internet Engineering Task Force (IETF) lists a tremendous number of low-level protocols that form the technological backbone of the Internet, but as developers began working with HTML and XML, the conversation moved beyond low-level BNF notation into a more accessible realm.

The popularity of the World Wide Web, specifically, HTTP, meant that virtually every major programming language soon included the ability to open a HTTP connection. Instead of engaging in the IETF-level semantics of a protocol, a developer could merely open a connection and get back data. XML, a stripped-down version of SGML, looked a lot like HTML but was easy to validate. A number of XML parsers were developed for a variety of languages, and suddenly, we could all move data back and forth very easily.

XML-RPC codified this notion into something that looks a lot more like a remote method call. Notice that there is no true object-oriented aspect to XML-RPC— no notion of inheritance or polymorphism, for example. This ensured that XML-RPC was accessible to nonobject-oriented systems, and that support would be available from a variety of systems.

SOAP, despite the original notion of "Simple Object Access Protocol," has over time acknowledged that it neither truly simple nor object-oriented, and the protocol officially no longer has any meaning (it's an acronym without an expansion). While the implementation of supporting libraries is more difficult, as we've seen it's not tremendously more difficult for a developer to either publish a SOAP service or use it.

The final addition of WSDL makes an application much easier to work with—as time has passed, virtually every modern development environment now has support for SOAP (at least as a client) and WSDL. Even such limited environments as Palm

OS (*http://www.palmos.com/dev/tech/webservices/*) and PocketPC (*http://www. pocketsoap.com/* or *http://msdn.microsoft.com/library/en-us/wcesoap/html/ceconSOAP. asp*) now support both SOAP and WSDL.

There will likely be a period of time in which an enterprising developer can offer bridge services between less mature services and the richer world of SOAP and WSDL (for example, it's easy to envision offering a SOAP view of the CDDB system). However, as of this writing, many of the organizations that currently offer non-SOAP systems (such as eBay) have already publicly indicated their desire to move to this environment.

The future of web services beyond SOAP and WSDL is far less clear. Some discuss the notion of choreography, which gives definition to the back and forth communication required to perform a transaction. Others point to a need for more coherence in terms of the actual APIs provided, or the details of what is meant by a transaction (for example, industry agreement over what is meant by a "purchase order" would make it easier to process an order across a supply chain). Savvy businesses and developers are too cautious to embrace a complex standard prematurely, and a lack of a clear, authoritative, credible organization has impeded efforts. Upon occasion, a very large organization is able to mandate a "standard" to partners, but typically these efforts are locked in as a proprietary system, not put forth as an open system.

It's not an accident that most of the popular systems (for example, XML-RPC, SOAP, and WSDL) have had complete implementations donated to a trusted, well known organization such as the Apache Group. Even if the software available isn't the best (although sometimes it is), a developer can work with the software, bundle it into their application, and otherwise take advantage of the "plumbing" provided without feeling encumbered by any potential proprietary system.

Probably the only real predication that can be made with any degree of certainty is the eventual coalescence of web services around SOAP and WSDL. Many of the services that don't implement SOAP already implement systems very closely. While SOAP and WSDL may never be as prevalent as HTTP and HTML, they will almost certainly eventually play as important a role in your development toolkit as TCP/IP or SQL.

Index

We'd like to hear your suggestions for improving our indexes. Send email to *index@oreilly.com*.

C

About the Author

Will Iverson has been working in the computer and information technology field professionally since 1990. His diverse background includes developing statistical applications to analyze data from the NASA Space Shuttle, product management for Apple Computer, and developer relations for Symantec's VisualCafé. For nearly five years, Will ran an independent J2EE consulting company with a variety of clients including Sun, BEA, and Canal+ Technologies. Will currently serves as the application development practice manager for SolutionsIQ. He lives in Seattle, Washington.

Colophon

Our look is the result of reader comments, our own experimentation, and feedback from distribution channels. Distinctive covers complement our distinctive approach to technical topics, breathing personality and life into potentially dry subjects.

The animal on the cover of *Real World Web Services* is a domestic pigeon (*Columba livia*). There are more than 150 breeds of domestic pigeon, in a variety of sizes, colors, and patterns. The typical domestic pigeon is distinguished by its blue and gray plumage. As adults, domestic pigeons are approximately 12 to 14 inches long and can weigh up to 3.5 pounds. Their traditional diet consists primarily of seeds and whole grains, and they can travel far from their nest to locate food. Domestic pigeons reach sexual maturity at five to seven months of age. They mate throughout the year but predominantly in the summer months. The female pigeon lays two eggs each mating cycle, and the male and female birds take turns sitting on the eggs to incubate them until they hatch.

The domestic pigeon is thought to be the first bird tamed by humans. The first domestic pigeons were bred about 6,000 years ago from the rock pigeon, which lived in the wild in Europe, the Middle East, and Southwest Asia. The domestic pigeon was first brought to North America in the early 1600s. Today, American domestic pigeons thrive in urban areas, where they have become comfortable amid the bustle and noise of city life and have adapted their diet to survive on leftover scraps of human food.

One of the most famous breeds of domestic pigeon is the carrier pigeon. Bred for the pigeon's exceptional homing abilities, the carrier pigeon has been used since ancient times to transmit written messages fastened to its body. When dispatched, the carrier pigeon can travel at a speed of 45 miles per hour, and despite traversing extremely long distances, it instinctively returns to its home coop. During World Wars I and II, carrier pigeons saved hundreds of human lives, intrepidly flying through combat zones to deliver crucial messages at times when radio transmissions weren't feasible.

Mary Anne Weeks Mayo was the production editor and copyeditor, and Sarah Sherman was the proofreader for *Real World Web Services*. Sanders Kleinfeld, Emily

Quill, and Claire Cloutier provided quality control. Mary Agner provided production assistance. John Bickelhaupt wrote the index.

Ellie Volckhausen designed the cover of this book, based on a series design by Edie Freedman. The cover image is a 19th-century engraving from the Dover Pictorial Archive. Clay Fernald produced the cover layout with QuarkXPress 4.1 using Adobe's ITC Garamond font.

Melanie Wang designed the interior layout, based on a series design by David Futato. This book was converted by Julie Hawks to FrameMaker 5.5.6 with a format conversion tool created by Erik Ray, Jason McIntosh, Neil Walls, and Mike Sierra that uses Perl and XML technologies. The text font is Linotype Birka; the heading font is Adobe Myriad Condensed; and the code font is LucasFont's TheSans Mono Condensed. The illustrations that appear in the book were produced by Robert Romano and Jessamyn Read using Macromedia FreeHand MX and Adobe Photoshop CS. The tip and warning icons were drawn by Christopher Bing. This colophon was written by Sanders Kleinfeld.

Related Titles Available from O'Reilly

Java

Ant: The Definitive Guide

Better, Faster, Lighter Java

Eclipse

Eclipse Cookbook

Enterprise JavaBeans,
4th Edition

Hardcore Java

Head First Java

Head First Servlets & JSP

Head First EJB

Hibernate:
A Developer's Notebook

J2EE Design Patterns

Java 1.5 Tiger:
A Developer's Notebook

Java & XML Data Binding

Java & XML

Java Cookbook, *2nd Edition*

Java Data Objects

Java Database Best Practices

Java Enterprise Best Practices

Java Enterprise in a Nutshell,
2nd Edition

Java Examples in a Nutshell,
3rd Edition

Java Extreme Programming
Cookbook

Java in a Nutshell, *4th Edition*

Java Management Extensions

Java Message Service

Java Network Programming,
2nd Edition

Java NIO

Java Performance Tuning,
2nd Edition

Java RMI

Java Security, *2nd Edition*

JavaServer Faces

Java ServerPages, *2nd Edition*

Java Servlet & JSP Cookbook

Java Servlet Programming,
2nd Edition

Java Swing, *2nd Edition*

Java Web Services in a Nutshell

Learning Java, *2nd Edition*

Mac OS X for Java Geeks

Programming Jakarta Struts
2nd Edition

Tomcat: The Definitive Guide

WebLogic:
The Definitive Guide

O'REILLY®

Our books are available at most retail and online bookstores.
To order direct: 1-800-998-9938 • *order@oreilly.com* • *www.oreilly.com*
Online editions of most O'Reilly titles are available by subscription at *safari.oreilly.com*

Keep in touch with O'Reilly

1. Download examples from our books

To find example files for a book, go to:
www.oreilly.com/catalog
select the book, and follow the "Examples" link.

2. Register your O'Reilly books

Register your book at *register.oreilly.com*

Why register your books?
Once you've registered your O'Reilly books you can:

- Win O'Reilly books, T-shirts or discount coupons in our monthly drawing.
- Get special offers available only to registered O'Reilly customers.
- Get catalogs announcing new books (US and UK only).
- Get email notification of new editions of the O'Reilly books you own.

3. Join our email lists

Sign up to get topic-specific email announcements of new books and conferences, special offers, and O'Reilly Network technology newsletters at:

elists.oreilly.com

It's easy to customize your free elists subscription so you'll get exactly the O'Reilly news you want.

4. Get the latest news, tips, and tools

www.oreilly.com

- "Top 100 Sites on the Web"—PC Magazine
- CIO Magazine's Web Business 50 Awards

Our web site contains a library of comprehensive product information (including book excerpts and tables of contents), downloadable software, background articles, interviews with technology leaders, links to relevant sites, book cover art, and more.

5. Work for O'Reilly

Check out our web site for current employment opportunities:

jobs.oreilly.com

6. Contact us

O'Reilly & Associates
1005 Gravenstein Hwy North
Sebastopol, CA 95472 USA

TEL: 707-827-7000 or 800-998-9938
(6am to 5pm PST)

FAX: 707-829-0104

order@oreilly.com
For answers to problems regarding your order or our products. To place a book order online, visit:

www.oreilly.com/order_new

catalog@oreilly.com
To request a copy of our latest catalog.

booktech@oreilly.com
For book content technical questions or corrections.

corporate@oreilly.com
For educational, library, government, and corporate sales.

proposals@oreilly.com
To submit new book proposals to our editors and product managers.

international@oreilly.com
For information about our international distributors or translation queries. For a list of our distributors outside of North America check out:

international.oreilly.com/distributors.html

adoption@oreilly.com
For information about academic use of O'Reilly books, visit:

academic.oreilly.com

O'REILLY®

Our books are available at most retail and online bookstores.
To order direct: 1-800-998-9938 • *order@oreilly.com* • *www.oreilly.com*
Online editions of most O'Reilly titles are available by subscription at *safari.oreilly.com*